SIMPLICITY

SIMPLICITY

Notes, Stories and Exercises
for
Developing Unimaginable Wealth

Mark A. Burch

NEW SOCIETY PUBLISHERS
Gabriola Island, BC   Philadelphia, PA

Canadian Cataloguing in Publication Data

Burch, Mark A. (Mark Alan), 1948-
  Simplicity

Includes bibliographical references.
ISBN 1-55092-268-8 (bound) — ISBN 1-55092-269-6 (pbk.)

1. Simplicity. 2. Conduct of life. 3. Life style. I. Title.
BJ1496.B87 1195   179'.9   C95-910412-7

Cover design by Val Speidel.

Book design and typesetting by Consensus Communications, Gabriola Island, BC.

Inquiries regarding requests to reprint all or part of *Simplicity: Notes, Stories & Exercises for Developing Unimaginable Wealth* should be addressed to:

New Society Publishers,
P.O. Box 189, Gabriola Island, B.C., Canada V0R 1X0,
or
4527 Springfield Avenue, Philadelphia PA, U.S.A. 19143.

Canada ISBN: 1-55092-269-6 (Paperback)
Canada ISBN: 1-55092-268-8 (Hardback)
USA ISBN: 0-86571-323-5 (Paperback)
USA ISBN: 0-86571-322-7 (Hardback)

Printed in Vermont on partially recycled paper using soy-based ink by Capital City Press.

To order directly from the publishers, please add $3.00 to the price of the first copy, and 75 cents for each additional copy (plus GST in Canada). Send check or money order to:

New Society Publishers,
P.O. Box 189, Gabriola Island, B.C. Canada V0R 1X0
or
4527 Springfield Avenue, Philadelphia PA, U.S.A. 19143.

New Society Publishers is a project of the Catalyst Education Society, a nonprofit educational society in Canada, and the New Society Educational Foundation, a nonprofit, tax-exempt public foundation in the U.S. Opinions expressed in this book do not necessarily reflect positions of the Catalyst Education Society nor the New Society Educational Foundation.

To my father, who helped me see.
To my mother, who helped me care.
To my children Aaron and Sarah to whom the future belongs.
To my friend Anne Camozzi, who helped me believe in my song.

CONTENTS

Acknowledgments

I would like to gratefully acknowledge permission from Harper Collins Publishers Ltd. to include the quotation from Edward Canze's *Buddhist Meditation* in this book. I would also like to thank Judith and Christopher Plant and the production staff at New Society Publishers for their gentle advice and continual encouragement.

—*Mark Burch, April 1995*

1
Living Simply

What is simplicity anyway?

What is simplicity anyway? The idea of the "simple life" evokes both nostalgia and dread. For some, living simply conjures up images of quaint, turn-of-the-century villages. This Hollywood imagery relates to a world and a lifestyle that probably never existed anywhere. But such depictions of simple living do help us recall some of the values associated with a less cluttered, hectic and complicated way of life. There was time to smell the roses. People enjoyed warmer and more trusting friendships and family bonds. Many people felt more deeply rooted in place and more continuity with history and heritage.

Nevertheless, many of these nostalgic images also include primitive and inefficient technology with questionable implications for human health. They also minimize the hardships and dangers endured by our ancestors. Communities may indeed have been closer in the last century, but much of this closeness grew from the collective need to meet the challenges of survival. People lived close to their birthplaces and stayed close to their "roots" as much from lack of the wherewithal to travel as from bonds of affection. In many cases, when economic progress liberated the denizens of small rural communities from the boredom and monotony of a parochial existence, they took the opportunity and explored new places. Moreover, when technology offered release from physical toil, these innovations were adopted as soon as possible.

Even the people of North America, for all their affluence and access to luxury, are still not many generations removed from the life of the pioneer, the colonist and the homesteader. We may romanticize this time in our history for emotional reasons, yet many of us associate the "simple life" with a technologically primitive lifestyle full of deprivation and toil. We desire a renewal of the human bonds we associate with the past and we deplore the loneliness and danger of modern cities. But most of us would not choose to gather nuts and berries for a living.

Our habit of thinking of simplicity either as stark deprivation or as nostalgic utopia causes us to miss the opportunity to explore and indeed *develop* meanings of simple living that involve neither destitution nor wishful thinking. Simplicity contains values that elude us if we maintain the prejudices and preconceived ideas supplied by the media and entrepreneurs whose vested interests lie in complexity and consumption.

In the following pages, I intend to explore the subject of simplicity, not as a romantic throw-back, but as a serious process of self-exploration and growth in mindfulness. I also want to discuss simple living as a wholistic, practical, individual response to many social injustices, ecological threats and economic insecurities. It is a path we can adopt in whatever degree we find congenial to our goals in life.

To begin, there are some things that I definitely do *not* mean by simplicity or simple living. These include false asceticisms that cause physical or emotional harm through deprivations of life's necessities; involuntary destitution suffered by people with long histories of oppression, exploitation or political instability; simplistic "back-to-the-land" movements based on complete naiveté concerning how complicated subsistence living really is(!); and moral élitism that equates poverty with virtue and innocence. I had only to meet two Franciscan monks who were in a bitter contest to see who could wear the shabbiest looking pair of shoes to realize that simplicity of spirit was something quite different from modest possessions.

First of all, voluntary simplicity is *voluntary*. It is a way of life that is chosen, not imposed. Circumstances of tragedy or privation may impose simplicity on us and this can be accepted more or less gracefully, but seldom is imposed poverty a joyful state. Voluntary simplicity, on the other hand, is an expression of human freedom one of whose objects is an increase in that freedom. Because it is chosen, it is joyous and powerful. Because it is chosen, it is an expression of self-esteem, self-confidence and a desire to flourish spiritually, emotionally and socially.

For this reason, nothing in the discussions that follow should be taken as some new apology for "happy poverty." While simplicity is joyous, poverty certainly is not. In singing the praises of simplicity, I am not offering some bromide that would maintain conditions of economic and social inequality. On the contrary, voluntary simplicity is exactly the sort of wholistic personal action that strikes at the roots of oppression, inequality and suffering.

Voluntary simplicity is a *matter of degrees*, not of meeting an absolute standard. If we point to examples of simple living such as the Greek philosophers Diogenes and Socrates, Jesus of Nazareth who had "no place to lay his head," Francis of Assisi or Henry Thoreau, it is only to define the yonder end of a journey that begins with ourselves, as we now live, where we now live. If I advocate simplicity it is not to urge that everyone live like a philosopher-ascetic, but rather to suggest a general direction for decisions that lead toward ever-increasing lightness of being. The life of the philosopher-ascetic, however romantic it may be, is hardly an option for most people who live in families, marriages or other relationships of mutuality.

In addition to being a matter of choice, voluntary simplicity implies moderation of material wants and redirection of activities. Duane Elgin has defined voluntary simplicity so that "to live more voluntarily means encountering life more consciously. To live more simply is to encounter life more directly."[1] The "directness" Elgin mentions refers to personal involvement in activities that are necessary to our life. It also implies heightened awareness of the existences of ourselves and of other creatures with whom we share the planet. It is a decision to forego the safety of second-hand experience for a riskier but more authentic involvement with life.

Like conservation efforts that reduce not what we *need* but what we *waste*, voluntary simplicity affirms every person's right to freedom from material want. It merely goes on to claim that the purposes of human life are more diverse and exciting than addictive materialism. Most of all, voluntary simplicity affirms human freedom and independence in the face of the powerlessness, dependency and despair that are the spiritual fruits of affluence.

In the following pages we will be exploring some of the many meanings of voluntary simplicity and reasons an individual or a family might embrace simplicity. Some reasons will be personal, while others have to do with spiritual values, social goals and ecologically sustainable living. Some of this ground has been mapped before by philosophers and essayists of previous centuries. We will not repeat this work or even offer a complete summary. Our purpose here is mainly to revive the flavor of these arguments and then move forward toward a technology of simplicity and the workbook exercises, which aim to build a mental and spiritual bridge from our present way of life into greater simplicity.

Much previous work on voluntary simplicity, beautiful as it is, has often left the *practice* of simplicity unexplored. Especially important is making the *transition* from a consumptive lifestyle to simplicity. In reading some of the previous work in this area, I get the impression it's merely a matter of throwing stuff out or giving it away, as if the transition must be made from affluence to simplicity in a single bound! My hope in developing the *Explorations* section of this book is to support this transition through exercises that help us develop mindfulness of the trade-offs required by our present way of living. Simple living is immensely rewarding for most people who practise it. But we must recognize and respect the great force of past learning and the incessant reinforcement of consumerism through the media, advertising and personal relationships. While there are undoubtedly some morally heroic souls who can "sell all, give to the poor, and follow him...," most of us have to travel toward this ideal of relationship in small, shaky steps. Many of us live within families or relationships wherein the generosities and compromises made for love often preclude radical individual actions. In these relationships, the choices we might make for ourselves need to be discussed with the partners, children and friends who might be affected by them. In so doing, we seek the common ground upon which we can both live according to our personal vision of simplicity and also in relationship with others.

So the *Explorations* section of this book addresses some of these issues by providing both a pathway for self-exploration and also a basis for discussion of major life decisions. These exercises can be done either alone, with a partner or in groups.

The third section of the book, *Simplicity Study Circles*, consists of a parallel set of exploration exercises designed specifically for use in groups. I have included some suggested agendas for short workshops, some group work guidelines and notes on doing workshops on voluntary simplicity.

Why voluntary simplicity?

Why would anyone want to adopt voluntary simplicity? Many answers have been offered over the years to this question. It deserves attention now no less than in the past.

Today we hear a lengthening litany of environmental, social, economic, political and spiritual threats to the future of humanity. For most people likely to read this book, reviewing the details of this situation will present nothing new. But an important point of departure for voluntary simplicity can be found in the idea that many problems facing humankind are *connected*. Environmental degradation, militarism, economic injustice, political unrest, social decay and a host of other issues seem to keep looping back on themselves in a single tangled mass. One develops the perspective not of a basically healthy people afflicted here and there by localized difficulties, but rather a people in basic difficulty blessed here and there with pockets of nearly unaccountable sanity and love.

People of goodwill are urged to confront this ball of maladies one affliction at a time, since the limitations of human intellect and energy seemingly preclude "solving" the whole mess at one go. We pick our issues in the hope that, together with others doing the same, we will somehow grope our way to a solution of the whole.

Intuitively, however, we wish for a more elegant way. The same intuition of the connections among problems hints at an equally wholistic response to dealing with them. Nature doesn't make new flowers by gluing a leaf here, a petal there; it produces *seeds*, which carry within themselves a principle of potentiality that can unfold into a complete new flower. If we cannot live with the harvest of our present way of making a living, we shall have to search for new seeds—values and perspectives so basic that they promise large pattern changes. The question then is what lies within the power of individuals to do to resolve this predicament?

So, to answer the question of why anyone would adopt voluntary simplicity, I offer some of my own thoughts as well as suggestions made by others, which I think fall into four broad groups: *personal, social, environmental* and *transpersonal (spiritual)* reasons.

Living simply for yourself

"A clay bowl as my only wealth, a robe that does not
  tempt the robbers,
Thus I dwell exempt from fear...."[2]

It's paradoxical that, on the one hand, Canada is one of the most desirable places in the world to live, and on the other hand, there is very considerable evidence of personal stress and discontent. Several surveys of job satisfaction in Canada have shown that a large number of people are unhappy with their work. Divorce rates, crime rates, substance abuse rates, assaults of all kinds, increasing child poverty, chronic problems with unemployment, prejudice and social unrest all suggest that in spite of living in an economically privileged country, many of us suffer dislocation and personal turmoil.

Voluntary simplicity is not a panacea for all of these problems. Nevertheless, a very large number of people are beginning to feel overwhelmed by the *pace* of life in North America as well as its *complexity*. North American society has been built on the assumption that more, bigger, and faster defines better, healthier and happier. Yet many of us have come to question this view. If achieving worthwhile goals requires that we must live at a manic pace, is it any wonder that we yearn for holidays when we then give ourselves permission to live according to the rhythms of our bodies and the cycles of the Earth?

Some years ago I went to an island in Lake of the Woods, northern Ontario, to attend a summer institute in bioenergetic therapy. About 30 people were left on the island for two weeks of intensive group therapy. Each of us, of course, had our personal issues to attend to, but what impressed me most was how healthy it was to be on the island. Intensive group work sessions as demanding as any work I had ever done were interspersed with music, sitting, massage, group housework chores, walking along the rocky shoreline of the island, listening to the lake lap at the dock, watching the loons and cormorants clamor about in the water, listening to each other's histories, dreams and nightmares. As the days passed, I began to slow down. Layer after layer of something burdensome was peeled back leaving me feeling open, sensitive, vibrant and energized. This process required nothing more than our presence in nature and our shared desire to attend to each other rather than to grand designs for changing the world or making a fortune.

I remember wondering why I couldn't just keep on living this way. We were not idle. There was ample time for productive work of some kind, yet it could be suffused with this same spirit of measured, attentive enjoyment of the moment. All that I had lived prior to the island experience seemed artificial and oppressive. I imagined that it may have been this quality that pervaded the lives of aboriginal people before their encounter with Europeans, a dream-like quality of union with nature and with each other, with one's *people*. How was it that we Europeans were so obsessed, so driven, so violent? What was it that so disturbed us that we felt driven to create a civilization (if it could be called that) such as now dominated North America?

I have lived for years very close to the Earth while homesteading in northern Ontario. I don't romanticize nature and I don't entertain any illusions about the hardships that aboriginal people must have endured. But I wonder if true wellness might lie somewhere *between* the rigors of a hunting and gathering lifestyle and breathing the canned air in the glass-walled cells of our highrise urban prisons.

To restate the question, it was not actually a matter of why life "couldn't" have more of an "island quality" about it. Beyond the broad archetypal patterns that define human nature, there is nothing in *life* which requires that it take a particular form. Rather, I realized, it was a matter of the *choices* we make that determine how much vitality and wellness we experience in the daily round. Changing these choices is within the power of individuals.

In a publication entitled *Personal Lifestyle Response to Social Injustice*,³ Jorgen Lissner offered ten reasons for choosing simplicity. Some of his arguments address personal reasons why we might adopt simple living. Lissner calls voluntary simplicity an *act of self-defence* against the mind-polluting effects of over-consumption. To live in North American society is to be, in one way or another, under attack. We are flooded every day with countless "messages," "offers," and "demands," most of which have to do with consuming things or services. The language of our economic system is the language of discontent. Its monotonous message is that this or that gewgaw is what we *do* need, or *will* need, or *ought* to have in order to be better, happier and more contented than we are now.

One of the clearest prophets of the Age of Consumerism was Victor Lebow writing in the *Journal of Retailing* in the mid-1950s:

> "Our enormously productive economy...demands that we make consumption our way of life, that we convert the buying and use of goods into rituals, that we seek our spiritual satisfaction, our ego satisfaction, in consumption.... We need things consumed, burned up, worn out, replaced, and discarded at an ever increasing rate."[4]

In the ensuing five decades, North Americans have taken Mr. Lebow's advice with a vengeance. Little has changed in the 1990s except for a few qualms about the environmental decay such a lifestyle has delivered.

Added to this voice of attraction is also a voice of warning: If we do not compete, purchase and accumulate, then our welfare will be undermined by other people trying to take it away from us (e.g., the Japanese, the Chinese, the Koreans, etc.), or by circumstances (e.g., economic recession, personal unemployment, debt, uncompetitiveness). So, if our hyperactivity cannot be stoked through manufactured discontent, we are threatened with manufactured images of loss and personal disaster.

This is not an emotionally or physically healthy climate for people. At the personal level, voluntary simplicity begins with the decision to take time to re-evaluate our activities and goals.

One of the definitions of stress is any form of *excessive demand*. We must experience some level of demand in our lives if we are to develop to our full potential. But each of us has a "comfort zone" where life's demands feel challenging rather than threatening. If this personal comfort level is exceeded then both emotional and physical symptoms can develop.

There are many kinds of demands. They can include *physical* demands such as unsatisfactory living conditions, hazardous work conditions, excessively laborious work, exposure to disease, shock, violence, threats of violence, and climatic extremes. We can also face *emotional* demands in relationships, at work, in our communities, families and friendships. *Intellectual* demands arise from the complexity of modern life, work requirements and the sheer quantity and muddle of information and decision-making we face each day. *Financial* demands arise as we try to match incomes with expenditures, finance college educations for our children, save for retirement, and reconcile the differing needs of family members. Finally, stresses from all of these sources can accumulate and reinforce each other.

All of this stress might be worth it if we could see clearly that it leads to higher quality of life and greater personal satisfaction. This is not the case, however. Surveys conducted ever since the 1950s have shown that while there has been a great increase in the pace and complexity of life, especially in urban centres, there has been no significant increase in perceived well-being. Personal consumption has approximately doubled since 1957, but the same proportion of people (about 30%) report being "very happy" with their lot in life now as in 1957.[5] Other research has shown that once incomes rise above the poverty level, there is little or no correlation between income level and well-being and that people from both rich, developed countries and "poor," developing countries often report comparable levels of personal well-being.[6] In some cases, people report being less satisfied with their lives now than in the past.

Voluntary simplicity offers a personal way of reducing stresses arising from lifestyles that have become too complex to be healthy or fulfilling. By living more simply we can increase financial security because less money is required and consequently a wider range of employment possibilities can provide an adequate income. By becoming more selective and conscious of our activities, we free time for family, friends and learning, which enhances our joy in life.

One of the ways that people who choose simplicity reduce demands in their lives is to apply energy selectively to those activities which make a direct contribution to livelihood and to do this, as much as possible, on a self-reliant basis or in partnership with neighbors. Meeting some of our own food needs by backyard gardening not only reduces the cash food budget, but increases self-confidence as we learn to produce and preserve our own food.

Working in partnership with friends and neighbors helps us discover our own skills and gifts as well as cementing bonds of interdependence. We rediscover that we need each other and can rely on each other. Security is then redefined not as the size of my bank balance but rather what I have to contribute to my community. Thus, simplicity finds security in *relationship* while consumerism seeks security in *ownership*.

The focus upon community that must characterize voluntary simplicity is another example of its rewards. We may be able to own and use things, but we don't have relationships with them. In many cases, the reward value claimed for the things we own comes to a focus in how they affect our relationships. The ostentatious car, the ever-changing wardrobe, the exotic cosmetics may find most of their reward value in the power we think they have to win social esteem, attention, and perhaps even love or sexual gratification. If we know how to experience social esteem, love and sexual gratification directly, why would we waste time on a flashy car?

Lissner also calls voluntary simplicity an *act of withdrawal* from the achievement-neurosis of our high-pressure, materialistic society. While this is true, I think we have to be clear on the meaning of "withdrawal." Voluntary simplicity is not a doctrine of niggardly hermithood! We don't withdraw from the existing socio-economic treadmill simply to sit and nurse our resentment against its misguided excesses. We withdraw from one pattern of behavior in order to adopt something else that is more life-giving. Like people striving to overcome addiction, we withdraw from self-destructive habits so that we can gain health and well-being. This takes time and usually requires community support.

For a number of years I helped organize spiritual retreats for men in my church community. The practice of retreat involves spending a weekend or more at a monastery or retreat centre in very simple surroundings with a minimum of socializing. Retreatants keep silence and attend to prayer, reflection, reading and rest. Most men from our congregation would not attend retreats and many of them expressed either anxiety at the thought of spending a night and two days in silence, or else they assured me they would be driven to distraction by the boredom of "nothing happening!" This was a real anxiety for many men and even those who attended retreats often found it impossible to sustain silence or solitude for more than a few hours.

This experience impressed me with how consistently our culture teaches us to passively focus our attention outwards rather than actively focus it inwards. The good consumer receives the world as entertainment. The more completely we are absorbed in this way of life, the less we believe in ourselves as active centres for the generation of consciousness, insight and joy. I don't believe that this is a collective *inability* so much as a *lack of training*.

On another occasion I made a solitary eight-day retreat during which my only conversation was a one-hour meeting with my retreat director once a day. One morning she said, "Just look and see God in all things." I thought this instruction was rather Zenish coming from a Benedictine abbess, but later that morning I sat in the monastery garden and watched a small, translucent green spider at work in a cotoneaster hedge. The days of silence before this morning helped me pay close attention to the spider. She worked methodically at spinning her web, caught an insect, paralysed it, wrapped it up in silk and fed upon it, then started repairing the web where her kill had struggled to get away. I watched all of this, deeply absorbed in it without actually *thinking* anything about it.

The spider simply *was*. And so was I. And we two were there together, absorbed together in the moment. When I was again aware of time, I realized that I had watched the spider for over an hour. I wasn't doing anything, exactly. But I felt that for a while, I had been caught up in something delicious and wonderful. Life was wonderful. Death was wonderful. The spider and the bush and the sun and I were all wonderful. Indeed, life was good and grace was everywhere. It occurred to me that I might spend several lifetimes this way considering how many flowers I could see bloom, how many webs, how many nests of birds and moulds and pond scums and leaves emerging on trees and butterflies emerging from chrysalises! Indeed. And what is human consciousness for?

We *withdraw* toward simplicity, then, not to become less but to become more, but in a different way from *having* more. What I think Jorgen Lissner means when he calls voluntary simplicity an "act of withdrawal" from achievement-neurosis is that it is both a movement *toward* a way of being that is deep and active and a differently directed consciousness. The achievement orientation of our culture chronically centres our attention on ourselves, our effort, our comfort, our cravings, our fears. Furthermore, it teaches us to locate both the source and the satisfaction of these states of consciousness outside ourselves. It is "other-centred" but only in a very special way—the way that serves the ends of the market economy. It does not allow the lingering, patient, focused and loving attention that can actually generate relationship.

A cluttered, complicated and consumption-oriented way of life leaves no time or energy for encounters with spiders, or other people for that matter. Another personal reason for adopting a simpler way of life is to dispose ourselves more often to such experiences. It is often in silence and solitude that we discover capacities for insight and joy that are intrinsic to our human nature, which cannot be bought and sold, and which preoccupation with buying and selling can actually silence.

A related aspect of all of this concerns the models of personal achievement behavior promoted by the mass media and corporate culture. The model professional is the person who can keep the most number of balls in the air at the same time: career, family, relationships, community, self-care, planetary well-being, gender issues, civil rights, healthy food, etc. He or she is wired to a computer, continually in motion, an international achiever, multilingual, always on the phone, always competent and achieving and somehow, miraculously, able to excel in all these categories. Especially for career-oriented women, the expectation seems to be to work fourteen-hour days at the same time as meeting personal and family needs and contributing to the community. This role model of the "modern" person is clearly manic. It is utterly devoid of repose, utterly devoid of depth, and more or less devoid of direction. We assume from all of this "busyness" that the man or woman in this picture is working hard for worthwhile goals, but we seldom know what they are. We are asked to accept that perpetual motion is its own reward, that the more one does the better, and if it can be done faster than anyone else, better still. The whole image is utterly antithetical to a measured, conscious and mindful approach to living. It is ideally suited, however, to the purposes of a corporate culture. Business wants highly mobile, image-oriented workers who can do its bidding anywhere in the world at any time.

In addition to reflecting on voluntary simplicity as an act of self-defence and an act of withdrawal, I would like to add another thought: that voluntary simplicity is an *act of affirmation*. Too often voluntary simplicity has the tone of puritanical renunciation, as if deprivation confers virtue. Simplicity sounds like an invitation to be cold and hungry and bored in atonement for some guilt we should feel for having been warm, fed and challenged. Little wonder that simplicity seldom appeals to many people.

Voluntary simplicity *is* an answer to many personal, social and environmental problems. But simplicity is not an end in itself. We may admire the clean lines of simple living just as we appreciate a Zen rock garden or an elegant mathematical proof. Yet neither of these aims to promote simplicity as such. Simplicity is a side-effect or precondition of working toward a deeper value.

The lives of people who embrace simple living display a passion for some deeper purpose from which power, possessions and the clutter of busy living represent distractions. Like freeing time to spend with a lover, lovers of simplicity free their lives of everything that might draw down their energy or obstruct the way toward their highest goals. For Jesus, it was proclaiming his Father's kingdom; for Socrates, it was the pursuit of Truth; for Thoreau, self-reliance and spiritual communion with his beloved New England; for Buddha, it was self-liberation. Though most of us keep less exalted company, we still know the pleasure of time with our children, our spouses, a craft or art form, the calling of our work or contributions we wish to make to our communities, which leave no room in our lives for excess baggage.

And here we find the evil of addictive acquisition: *that it distracts us from what is best in our lives*. Voluntary simplicity brings us nothing of its own, but it clears a space within which we can rediscover and honor our highest loves. It may be that we choose personal simplicity because of the benefits it brings to the planet and to other people. Yet these benefits must bring us personal satisfaction as well.

Thus, for many of us, the pathway to simplicity will not be found through feeling guilty about what we own. A surer route is remembering when we have felt the most profound joy and fulfilment in our humanity. These moments are still possibilities for the future. Finally, falling in love with what is truly worthy of our love, we claim the courage to dispense with whatever would cause us again to forget and go back to sleep. We simplify only partly to atone for the guilt of over-consumption. More crucial is that we shed clutter as we shed clothing to be with a lover, to be close, to join, to merge and be joyful.

Simplicity is not prerequisite to a meaningful life; it is co-requisite to it. Simplicity enables mindfulness and mindfulness enables peace and delight. The more we find our peace and delight in simplicity and mindfulness, the more completely we embrace them. Simplicity, mindfulness and peace arise gradually and together as co-requisite aspects of a self-strengthening pattern. The more they are chosen and coexist, the less room remains in our lives for unthinking hyperactivity. Voluntary simplicity is good because it makes possible attentive devotion to those experiences that define our fullest humanity rather than conferring on someone else a maximum of wealth. Only a simple life can be concentrated mindfully upon its art— whatever "art" that may be. Only a simple life is free enough from distraction to focus deeply upon its sacred goals without haste or diversion. Only a simply life can lay hold of inner riches.

Voluntary simplicity can also be an *act of self-enrichment* in that living simply, we realign our involvements away from things and toward self, other people and the ecosphere. One of the fruits of simple living is time. But clearly, we aren't here merely to vegetate! We naturally want to use the time for something. We meet the difference between simplicity and consumerism precisely at this point: given some time, how shall I use it? Modern society allows us to face this question only very rarely because most of our time is structured for us by the demands inherent in a wasteful, consumption-oriented way of life. Many people have trouble planning a holiday without money. In fact, we may even save money all year so that our holidays become special occasions for over-consumption!

Consciously deciding how to use time is something that is usually connected with crises in our lives such as unemployment, completing a higher education and searching for a first job, retirement, holiday planning, or some forced life change like an illness that imposes the need to radically restructure our use of time. Simple living implies making conscious decisions about how we use more and more of our time and orienting our activities around the goals we find most satisfying and meaningful. Exercises in the second part of this book are designed to assist with this process.

About a year ago I decided to begin learning T'ai-chi. I went through all the usual self-doubts, wondering if I could learn a martial art in mid-life, wondering if I could even remember all the moves in the set, wondering if I could develop the self-discipline to stay with it long enough to learn it. On the other hand, I loved watching T'ai-chi and admired anyone who could do it. To me, it embodied some of the grace and eroticism of ballet, the spirituality of Taoist meditative practice and the "shadow" of deadliness that is one of the meanings of any martial art.

Practising T'ai-chi became wholly absorbing. It has been remarkable how something so apparently simple continues to reveal complexities and subtleties I could never have guessed by watching someone else do it. T'ai-chi has been a little like love-making. It is so *intrinsically* pleasurable that I want to do it over and over again. While I was learning the set, I was mentally reviewing the movements even when I wasn't practising with my body. One night, I awakened from doing the "crane cools wings" movement in my sleep! T'ai-chi had an "island" flavor to it and renewed the question in my mind: why are things like this, the mainstays of life, marginalized by our culture?

T'ai-chi continues to reveal benefits and levels of inner transformation as I muddle along with the practice of it. But its most important lesson for me was the realization that as I moved through the steps of the set, nothing was being consumed or owned. I was nothing, moving through nothing, shaping nothing in the fillings and emptyings, the expansions and contractions, the scoops and pushes of T'ai-chi. T'ai-chi is invisible until it enters someone's body. It does nothing to harm the ecosphere. It does nothing to oppress anyone else. You cannot own T'ai-chi. You don't need any fancy equipment or designer body suit to practise T'ai-chi. And yet doing it floods the senses and consciousness with subtle intuitions and knowings, many of which are impossible to describe in words. Now, no day feels complete without doing at least one T'ai-chi set.

Learning T'ai-chi was a form of self-enrichment. Lately I have moved along to begin teaching others what I learned and, I hope, to enrich their lives as well. My own practice of simplicity is as halting and inconsistent as anyone's. But I can see deepening that practice in my life would open time and energy for more study of T'ai-chi and disciplines like it.

To conclude, I would suggest that for many people voluntary simplicity might be an *act of moral consistency*.

Most people likely to read this book probably will not be directly or personally involved in the oppression of workers in developing countries, military dictatorships, unfair labor practices or massive ecological destruction. But one of the paradoxes of our century is the discontinuity between our personal moral codes and *systemic evil*, which arises from collective patterns of action or inaction. I may not be personally responsible for the jailing or torture or execution or exploitation of other people, yet I participate in and indirectly support economic and political systems that do these things.

While our individual responsibility to change oppressive systems is clear, our *power* to make a difference is largely determined by the positions of formal authority we hold in such systems. Needless to say, for those of us who have no formal position of power, the circumference of realistic personal action is measured by the choices we make in personal lifestyle issues.

I would suggest that much of the political and ecological oppression occurring in the world today is directly or indirectly linked to our economic system. This system distributes costs, benefits and wastes very unfairly. It is inherently misdirected in maintaining stark social and economic inequalities while trying to orient human consciousness toward dependency and consumerism as definitions of the "good life."

But personal action toward voluntary simplicity falls well within the circle of steps that fit our walk more closely to our talk. Voluntary simplicity focuses our life energies specifically on actions that have little inherent power to exploit or oppress others. The emphasis in simple living upon self-reliance and community helps assure that basic personal needs will be met close to home in solidarity with friends and neighbors. This in turn implies that *how* we meet our needs will be more closely linked to our sphere of personal action and personal responsibility wherein we *do* have the power to act with moral consistency. Furthermore, as we withhold even our indirect support and participation from the dominant economic system, we do a little bit to weaken its power to project systemic evil elsewhere in the world.

We will now turn more specifically from the personal reasons for embracing simplicity to all those reasons that relate to our lives together in society. Voluntary simplicity can be a powerful antidote to social and economic injustice.

Living simply for others

See us go the fool's way
gathering all about us
for a covering, a surety,
a pleasure;
Opiates to fill time's hollow;
piles of things which rot away
or linger near our ankles
to stop us dancing.

Our time in history is marked by extreme differences in material well-being. One-fifth of the Earth's people consume four-fifths of its resources to support lifestyles of affluence while the least advantaged one-fifth live in rags, starvation and illness. Individual extremes of wealth and poverty are even more pronounced.

The moral unacceptability of this situation is recognized nearly everywhere, yet no society, including the most affluent, has eradicated destitution. In many cases, the affluence for the minority literally requires the involuntary impoverishment of the majority because of the centralizations, trade inequities and environmental exploitation required to deliver riches to the privileged.

Part of the reason for the persistence of such injustice can be found in the approach we have taken to redressing poverty. When one group has more and another less, there are basically two ways that greater equality can be attained. The first approach is the one that has formed the mainstay of economic thinking in northern countries. Those with less will acquire more, the theory goes, if the economy can grow. Economic growth is the proposed solution for the hardships of destitution.

In spite of enormous growth in the world economy, however, there is more poverty now than ever before. Economic growth tends to benefit those who are already in privileged positions at the expense of the poor and of the ecosphere. While growth sounds good in theory, in practice the capital needed to create growth is controlled by a minority, which in turn reaps the profits from its investment. Total wealth increases, but its distribution becomes more unequal. In addition, it is clear that there are ecospheric limits on the total scale of human economic activities.

In this context, the choice to live simply becomes an *act of sharing*. Sharing is the alternative to growth. A cynic might say that the emphasis placed on growth by economists is merely a way of trying to avoid or delay sharing. If the total economic pie can be made to grow, then I don't have to share my piece with you. We can make your piece bigger.

Sharing means that if you are to have more, I must have less. When what I think I *am* is mostly defined by what I *have*, sharing is a particularly threatening prospect. Offering to share what I own becomes "giving up" what I *am*. Sharing one's material possessions is then a partial or total loss of identity, power, privilege and self.

Expressing it this way emphasizes what an absurd cul-de-sac we have engineered. Having does not define being, as ten seconds of introspection reveals. But market economies teach us to associate the consumption of goods and services closely with non-material states of consciousness and feeling that do define being. It takes a considerable act of self-awareness to disentangle the two. The result is that the idea of *having* less, no matter how just the cause, *feels* to us like *being* less.

Simplicity offers a way of redefining the self that confers

a great freedom from this anxiety. The choice for simplicity only requires "giving up" in order to share in the first stages of the transition from affluence to simplicity. Little is needed when we define our character and presence in the world in other ways than through material acquisition. Sharing is difficult for those who already think they have much and must relinquish what they have. For the one who has and needs little, there is always abundance of what is needed and in this abundance, a measureless sense of security.

Because simplicity is the choice to live lightly in the world, it foregoes the use of resources, which then become available to help meet the needs of others. Non-use of material things is an indirect but extremely effective way of sharing that is within the immediate power of every individual. Living in material simplicity also frees time and energy that otherwise would have been devoted to the acquisition, maintenance and disposal of possessions. One is at liberty to take pleasure in life, friendships, and in pursuing goals that are intrinsically rewarding.

Advocates of economic growth will say this argument is naive. They will point to the synergies in technological and economic development that aims at growth. They will argue that it is precisely because we have had a growth-oriented economic system that encourages individuals to increase personal gain that discoveries have been multiplied and the overall economic and social good has increased. Many of these same people will argue that growth in military production is also good because the defence industry has often been responsible for technical innovations that have eventually found their way into civilian production. As if human beings simply lose their inclination to create unless driven by threats of invasion or by the lust for nationalistic self-aggrandizement!

Whether or not a growth-oriented economy has fostered synergies that have spurred technological progress, *in any case* this process is now reaching ecological and social limits. It is naive in another sense to believe that because of its synergistic history, economic and technical development somehow occurs in a sealed vessel that is unaffected by the social, cultural, ecological and spiritual dimensions of livelihood. An excellent recent example of this principle is the report of the Royal Commission on Reproductive Technology, which recommended a number of constraints on the development and application of such technology based on social, psychological and moral considerations. While we may not be able to identify limiting factors *within* the process of technical creativity, we can certainly define some that characterize the living world as a whole. Our technical and economic system cannot continue producing ever-widening social inequities of power and privilege, or ever-widening chasms between the demand for resources and energy, without regard for the capacity of the planet to provide ecological services and resources.

Similarly, living simply can be an *act of sustainable development*. There has been much discussion, much of it confused, around the issue of "sustainable development," which is often freely interchanged with "sustainable economic growth."

Growth means quantitative expansion in scale, size or number. Northern, industrialized, "developed" nations cannot stand any more growth, nor can the planet support it. If human cultures everywhere on Earth are to sustain themselves over the long term, growth must cease and the pursuit of growth as a means to riches must cease.

Development refers to qualitative or functional

improvement. It is an inherently value-laden concept. It refers to changes that are desired and valued. Development is clearly possible in a steady-state, non-growing system.

The confusion of growth with development provides fertile ground for sophistry and manipulation. Those who promote growth can easily confuse and discredit people who question growth as a good means of achieving development. They make their opponents appear to be against progress and development when they question the value of growth.

One way to expand the distinction between growth and development is to note that development usually works to the good of the whole, of all species, and all participants in the development process. Growth, on the other hand, always involves "trade offs," finding a "balance," which usually means everyone loses something, and "breaking eggs to make omelets," which usually means degradation of ecosystems.

Growth degrades environments and communities. Development enhances and enriches them through an increase in variety, diversity, functional integration and interdependence, a deepening of relationships—but all of this without growth in scale, quantity or number.

Voluntary simplicity is all about sustainable development. That is, it is about long-term qualitative improvement in the human lot, which can be pursued indefinitely.

Simplicity is definitely not about growth for its own sake, sustainable economic growth, environmentally sustainable growth, sustainable wealth, or any other self-contradictory notion.

If reasons for living more simply include acts of sharing and sustainability, Jorgen Lissner has suggested that simplicity is an *act of solidarity* in community with others. Our personal choice to live simply places us in the company of those who have no choice. Acts of solidarity are expressions of both political consciousness and social affirmation. Such expressions are particularly significant when we have a real choice. To live simply because of misfortune or accident of birth is to endure one of the darker sides of fate. But to live simply as a matter of choice is to affirm the value of non-material goals in life and to bring our warmth and creativity to the world of constraints and limitations that shapes the lives of people who must live with circumstance. If life is in any way a matter of "taking sides," and many spiritual mentors have suggested that it is, then simplicity as an act of solidarity declares our decision to side with the mass of humanity such as it is, rather than the values and lifestyles of the privileged.

Finally, simplicity as an act of solidarity declares to those of slender means that a life of material affluence doesn't always deliver all that it promises. The most successful feature of international development projects has not been transferring technology to the developing world, eradicating disease, alleviating illiteracy or establishing social and political justice. The greatest success of international development efforts since the 1950s has been to thoroughly diffuse the North American obsession with affluence into every other culture it has touched. Now, not only do we live the unsustainable paradox of 20 per cent of the world's people producing 80 per cent of its ecological damage and waste, we have the remaining 80 per cent of humanity clamoring to live the same way. The choice for simplicity declares by example that not everyone in North

America is prepared to admire the emperor's new clothes.

I agree with Lissner that simplicity as an act of solidarity can also be *provocative* of dialogue on the values that guide the development of our societies and our families, *anticipatory* of the day when the majority of people who have been disenfranchised from affluence will make their just claims to a share of Earth's resources, and an act of *advocacy* for a cultural and economic order that is more equitable and life-giving.

Voluntary simplicity is also an *exercise of purchasing power*. Many of us live from pay cheque to pay cheque without ever attending very closely to the considerable financial power we exercise as individuals. Consider that someone employed for 40 years with a median income of perhaps $40,000 per year will be making daily decisions during that period that deploy $1.6 million. Some practitioners of simplicity will trade income for time. Others will find opportunities in their careers to make meaningful contributions in service of values they cherish, but may divert some part of their income to non-material purposes.

Whatever income is earned must eventually be spent somehow. Exactly how it is spent has a profound effect on the shape of our economy and society. For all its faults and injustices, our economy is exquisitely sensitive to market demand or the lack of it. When demand disappears for a product or service, so does the product or service. Great strides have been made in the technology of artificially creating demand for products and services that have no relation to basic human needs, or for needs that could be met much more directly in some other way. The success of the market economy and its oppressive effects on the human spirit in North America can be found in how often shopping is a substitute for a social life, *the* major antidote to boredom, a significant way to express feelings of power and control, an important opportunity to socialize and experience sensory stimulation, and the purchases resulting from it are major surrogates for self-esteem.

The choice for simplicity implies making decisions regarding how we dispose of personal income through purchasing or, as the case may be, refraining from purchasing certain goods and services. Some general principles that can help guide these decisions have been suggested by the Simple Living Collective of San Francisco. These principles are reviewed in the *Explorations* section of this book, but come down to relating our purchasing decisions directly to basic needs and activities that enhance personal independence and reduce social and international oppression.

Less obvious perhaps is the idea that voluntary simplicity is an *act of nonviolence*. Most of the time, we are not directly aware that the right to possession is maintained by violence, but it is only thinly concealed by time and distance. At the physical level, the production of any material object often requires the cutting, grinding, tearing, milking, dismembering, uprooting, crushing, heating, freezing, etc. of some living or formerly living thing. What we make is literally built of the corpses of other beings. It is not my purpose to sentimentalize this violence because it is a violence that is inherent in all living things that rely on other living things for their life. I only wish to point out that at the physical level, the decision to maximize one's possessions necessarily requires maximizing this kind of violence.

Equally important, however, is the realization that the illusion of possession implies violence between people. In fact, no one can really possess anything. We appear in the world naked and we disappear from it equally naked. During our brief tenancy here, we can attempt to claim the more or less *exclusive* right to use certain things, enjoy their properties, and dispose of them as we please, but we don't really possess them. Thus, possession, having, owning, are merely words describing a set of social arrangements that confer rights of use and disposal upon some individuals to the exclusion of other individuals. Such arrangements are not always agreeable among all parties in society and then the *enforcement* of exclusive rights of use and disposal comes to involve the coercive power—i.e. violence—of the state. The implied threat of violence or its actual application is thus the social force that supports ownership. To try to "own" something is to participate, more or less, in this system. The more I claim to own, the more I participate.

Evidence of this is everywhere. There is a disturbingly direct relationship between increasing material wealth and security systems. The larger the house, the more expansive the grounds, the bigger the office building, the more we see surveillance cameras, fences, alarms, dogs and guns. Where very great wealth is concerned, these tools of violence and this evidence of fear is well-concealed and manicured into the landscape but a single breach, no matter how innocent, brings it into clear view.

We recognize yet a deeper meaning of "ownership." While it is true that the coercive power of the state enforces property "rights," many thoughtful people see a basis for this right that is intrinsic to human nature. That is, if I, by my effort and ingenuity, transform some trees into lumber and the lumber into a house, my right to claim exclusive possession of the house derives from my labor and my creativity. Had I not applied my talents thus, the house would not exist. Since it does exist through my constructive activity, it is said to belong to me. Some would argue that it is this relationship between a human being and the fruits of labor that constitutes ownership and that we authorize the state to protect.

But even here, the claim to "have" something that we have made is tenuous at best. It positions the human worker on a par with Divine Being, as if we made things out of nothing. Again, what we actually do is claim temporary user rights over materials that have been loaned to us from the heart of another, truly creative mystery. Who knows, *really*, how the tree grows? Who can make it grow when it will not, or make it grow thus and not so? And from whence comes our insight, our creativity, our ability to solve problems and hatch new plans? Are we not actually *recipients* of mysterious materials, mysterious abilities and marvellous powers? Do we not, in fact, *rearrange* elements of creation we neither make nor unmake?

From this perspective, we must be more tentative in crying "Mine!" In choosing simplicity, we further the growth of consciousness by appreciating life as gift rather than personal accomplishment. We recognize ownership as a human convention born in fear and violence, fear that we will lack something we need and violence to assure its supply, which has no cosmic basis. We then become less prone to endorse the use of violence against others to protect "rights" that have no foundation in being.

Closely related to the capacity of the state to exercise coercive violence to maintain property rights is the extension of this violence to war-making. With the dissolution of the Soviet Union and the relaxation of East/ West tensions, much of the drive behind the post-Second World War peace movement has now dissipated. Yet war and the preparation for war continues to be a major preoccupation of many countries. The conflict in the Persian Gulf demonstrated that conventional war-making is just as destructive in both human and ecological terms as nuclear war might be. The Persian Gulf example is particularly apposite to voluntary simplicity since a major reason for North American involvement in that conflict was to assure the stability of oil prices.

While many conflicts around the world are local or regional battles related to nationalistic goals within the countries concerned, conflicts that involve North Americans have invariably been related to protecting economic interests. The lifestyle of affluence and consumption that is widely promoted in our society contributes directly to these military adventures.

Moreover, research and development activities for military purposes still largely dominate the attention of the scientific and technological establishment. Military spending still consumes a very large fraction of global wealth and resources each year while the production, use and disposal of this equipment serves no life-giving purpose.

The debate over whether or not armies are still required in today's increasingly interdependent world will likely go on for some time. What seems clear, however, is that the present level of military production and spending are unsustainable. In addition, to the extent that individuals begin to choose simple living and the overall resource and energy intensity of our economy is reduced, the motivation for military overdevelopment will be reduced as well. While military institutions may never completely disappear, it would be all gain if they could be scaled back to vestigial replicas of the monsters that are still so much with us.

Militarism is a global issue with systemic roots. The individual decision to live more simply clearly will not reverse the trend to militarization of economies and societies. But as we mentioned before, individual decisions do matter when many individuals take similar decisions. Thus, another major reason for simple living is the hope that by supporting each other in this choice we will eventually build sufficient social momentum for systemic as well as individual change.

Should this transition occur, then the opportunities for people in other regions and countries to become more autonomous in their development would greatly increase. Money and resources that are now going into arms purchases and defence would become available for local development. Savings from arms expenditures would also be available for expanding our knowledge and appreciation of the universe, for the exploration and colonization of space, and for the alleviation of much human misery.

I would now like to consider some of the reasons for simple living that relate to our place within the ecosphere.

Living simply for the Earth

In the summer of 1989, prairie Canada sweltered in blistering drought. We had had several years of below average rainfall. The water tables had dropped substantially. The Assiniboine River, which curls its way through the community where I lived, looked like a muddy ditch with a disturbingly slender trickle of water moving slowly through its midline.

One afternoon in July, I was returning to work from my lunch break. The wind was up and the temperature around 35 Celsius. All the grass in the city had long since turned brown and the trees rustled their foliage with a serpentine hiss. The wind seemed like a blast furnace and the sun beat down, not with the friendly warmth of childhood memory, but with the ferocity of a blow torch. Everywhere dust was beginning to cloud the air, caking vehicles, buildings and people. It gave a gritty, choking quality to the air that seized me in the throat at the same time as it threatened to sand the skin from my face.

In spite of how inclement it was, I stood there absorbed in feeling the elements whirl around me. For a moment, I felt that the whole Earth had turned hostile toward me—toward us. Like a child in relation to his mother, I sometimes felt that mother was being unpleasant, yet I never questioned her basic love for me. But on this day in July, something shifted. I wondered whether this was the beginning of global warming, or if this was what it would be like when it was well under way. Like everyone else in the 20th century, I probably carried some dismal forebodings about such an event, but also like everyone else, I kept it safely suppressed beneath layers of routine, wilful ignorance and what the Trappist monk Thomas Merton once called "sunshine and uplift." This day, however, the weather broke through my psychological evasions. I experienced *in my body* some premonition of what it would be like for us if the planet changed in ways that rendered human life difficult or impossible to sustain.

Of course I don't personify nature and I don't believe nature can "have it in" for human beings. When I experienced in that moment an ecosphere that had turned hostile rather than nurturant, what I actually experienced was a psychological projection of my own guilt for causing environmental damage. This is a very ancient sort of feeling, the feeling that the "gods" have become angry because of human wrongdoing or greed. It was a very archetypal feeling. In a sense, my unconscious was saying, "Look, if you keep living this way, this is what you deserve...the wrath of nature. This is simple justice; cause and effect; the wages of sin. It's nothing personal and yet it's very personal. This is the way things are. Wise up or perish."

Human beings can live only because we consume other creatures for food, clothing and shelter. We change the natural world, rearranging its materials, its species and landscapes, to meet our needs. This is an inescapable requirement of our being. We develop culture and technology to help us get along in the world, rather than undergoing physical change. This capacity has enabled us to inhabit nearly every bioregion on earth.

But we exploit the ecosphere not only for what we *need*, also for what we *want*. As our numbers grow, so do our needs. And as our desires increase, so does our exploitation of the ecosphere. Our economic system now manufactures not only the products to satisfy our desires, it also manufactures desires for its products. Paradoxical as it sounds, our economic system no longer operates to satisfy human craving and deliver contentment, but rather, it operates to multiply cravings and discontentment. Only unhappy and discontented people consume more than they need.

It is unlikely that any future technology will reverse these relationships: the more people and the more wants, the greater the impact on the ecosphere. The relationships are probably not linear, but they will always remain direct and positive. We have little choice in the matter.

Within the obvious requirement of our being to exploit the ecosphere to *some* degree, exactly to *what* degree *is* a matter of choice.

Historically, our impact on the biosphere has degraded it. When our numbers were few, technology simple, and world view animistic, we occupied certain regions for a very long time indeed. But in the case of hunter-gatherer societies, our damage to the Earth was within its capacity to heal itself. The point is that even in societies where the prevailing value is not that of personal accumulation of material goods, human activities more or less always reduce biological diversity, degrade soils, reduce forest cover and leave behind waste.

Where human numbers are large, technology powerful and world views materialistic, our impact on the ecosphere is catastrophic.

In facing the environmental emergency of the late 20th century, we have been encouraged to "Reduce, Reuse, Recycle and Recover," with most emphasis on recycling. Recycling is popular because it promises consumption without guilt. It allows the free market economic machine to continue operating with only minor adjustments to its input and output cycles. Recycling never requires that we cease doing a thing, only that we do the same thing differently.

But until someone discovers a way to reverse the laws of physics, recycling will reduce but never overcome our degradation of environments. It is possible, however, to minimize the degree and extent of degradation. This is accomplished by the "first R," the one that gets the least attention. Whenever we reduce our demand for resources and energy, pollution and consumption of resources are avoided.

This goal can be approached in two ways, both of which can be practised together. First, we can reduce demand for resources by *reducing waste*. Waste reduction stresses efficiency while leaving goals unquestioned. We live the same way, value the same things, pursue the same goals, but we use methods and technologies that reduce the wastage of energy and resources in the process. This is the conservationist approach to environmental protection and stewardship of resources. It is also essentially the approach advocated by "sustainable development."

Another way to reduce demand is to *reduce consumption* in an absolute sense. This involves a review of basic life goals, how we spend our time, talents and treasure, and the role accorded to material consumption as a means to pleasure, health, self-esteem or public reputation. To the extent that we live simply, we conserve the planet that is our home.

Clearly, we can both reduce waste and consumption. We can continually reassess our goals at the same time that we try to pursue them with as little waste as possible. The choice for voluntary simplicity thus becomes the most direct, personal and powerful individual *act to conserve the ecosphere and all its creatures.*

Even if we take a selfish perspective, the choice for simplicity and conservation is *an act to enhance our quality of life* in the present by enhancing the healthfulness of the natural environment. Human beings cannot flourish in degraded environments. To choose simplicity is to choose to care not only for the natural world, but in caring for it, to care for ourselves.

Thus simplicity reverses the maxim of the consumer society, that consumption defines quality of life. Rather, we assert that we are rich in proportion to the things we can afford to do without. As practitioners of simplicity, we respond to the question "What have my grandchildren ever done for me?" with "Caring for the world that my grandchildren inherit is another way of caring for myself." And to the challenge "In the long run, we're all dead" we would reply, "No. In the long run, we're all connected."

Naturally, we will want to assure that even those things we do choose to acquire, as well as the things we need, will be manufactured with as little degradation to the ecosphere as possible. A great challenge to human creativity will be the development of ever more efficient and benign technologies for meeting human needs and aspirations. This challenge will never end. But the choice for simplicity recognizes that only a limited part of our human potential can be realized in terms of the possession and consumption of material things.

If voluntary simplicity is ever widely adopted, it will imply a much simpler economy and a different direction for technological development. It does not necessarily imply poverty and technical primitivity. Economic activity would become more focused on meeting essential human needs directly and efficiently. Technological development would be directed not toward the generation of wealth, but toward the generation of *wisdom* and *well-being*. And there would not, of course, be any role at all for technologies intended for war, for oppression of other people, or for self-interested exploitation of the planet for personal gain.

I would suggest therefore, that voluntary simplicity is

the most immediate and direct pathway for individuals to reduce waste; reduce demand for energy and resources; conserve habitats and species; assure quality of air, soil and water resources; and help maintain our planetary stocks of natural resources for future generations and the economically disadvantaged members of humanity who are already with us.

Living simply more deeply

We've now explored many reasons for choosing simplicity, some of which are perhaps obvious and have been mentioned by other authors in the past, and some of which may have been less obvious or less well-explored. In several places I have suggested that embracing simplicity involves a shift in attention, and often a shift in "love interest" if such a phrase can be permitted, from preoccupation with the physical, material and consumptive aspects of life to "other goals," without really saying much about what these other goals might be.

Simplicity is often connected with spiritual development. This is the case because the spiritual unfolding of personality requires such singleness of purpose, clear attention, dedication of energy and unwavering intent that monastic expressions of spirituality have left little room for materialism or the complexities of a "worldly" orientation to life. In some dualistic spiritual traditions, maintaining psychological, emotional or physical attachments to material possessions or entertaining the desire to accumulate them were associated with sin, evil, or at best, with ignorance about the nature of the world and how such attachments could become impediments to spiritual development.

While these arguments may be true and valid, they have received much more insightful and eloquent treatment by past writers than I could ever hope to bring to the discussion. I don't want to treat the spiritual dimension of simplicity purely as a call to religious asceticism or austerity, though for some it may bring them much reward.

Instead, I would suggest that the choice for simplicity can first of all be an *act of shifting attention from the quantitative aspects of things to their qualitative aspect*. Without forsaking in any way the enjoyment of our senses and our involvement with the physical and material aspects of the universe, we can yet change *how* we are present to these transactions.

A consumptive approach to existence is one that focuses attention on the outer aspects of life, on the number and quantity of things owned or consumed, and on the range or variety of possessions or property amassed. To have much is to be much. To have options, to have accumulated and controlled the largest, the most, the greatest extent or degree of whatever thing we are using at the moment, defines well-being.

Simplicity, however, is the choice to shift attention toward the *quality and depth* of our relationships with things rather than their number or extent. We do not eschew the getting and having of material possessions. But we do concentrate on becoming more conscious of *why* we are choosing to own something, the *extent* of its usefulness, the *fullness* of our enjoyment and use of it, and the *effects* that it has on our lives. To own the world's largest collection of guitars is one way of defining well-being. To own one guitar that we have learned to play with great sensitivity and expertise is another way of defining well-being, one which stresses the qualitative aspect of our relationship to the instrument. The choice for simple living is increasingly to attend to these qualitative aspects of our existence.

Some years ago I developed a fairly serious case of pneumonia. As my fever increased, I lost my appetite, and perhaps my judgment. I spent several days in a fevered state essentially without eating or drinking much at all. As fasting interacted with the fever, some fairly strange "altered states" began to pervade both my waking hours and my sleep. After about six days of this, it was evident that I was very sick indeed and I finally presented myself for medical attention. One bottle of antibiotics and a stern lecture later, I was back home in bed and decided to force some fluids along with the medication.

I poured a glass of very cold apple juice and brought it to bed with me. I sipped the juice very slowly and was utterly stunned by the delicious, wine-like quality of the drink. It was the most savory and luscious delight! How had I missed this so often? Surely, this was the same juice I had always enjoyed, but what was so different this time? Clearly, it was *me*. I was paying attention to the juice. I had nowhere else to go, nothing else on my mind, and a clean palate from five days of fasting. But the point was that the apple juice itself must always have had these delightful qualities. I was only now paying attention to them—deep, mindful attention. The *quality* of drinking the juice was now more important than the quantitative experience of simply quenching my thirst. In that moment, sick as I was, I wondered why this sort of mindful attentiveness could not suffuse all of life's experiences.

The choice for simple living represents another shift for many people and that is the shift from attending to the outer, physical, material and objective aspects of our lives *toward the inner, psycho-emotional, non-material and subjective side of living*. This is a logical result of giving less time and attention to the clutter and complication that goes with owning many "toys." To the extent that I fill my life with earning, saving, buying, cleaning, maintaining, disposing, repurchasing, operating and repairing many "things," there is relatively less energy available for attending to subjective, intuitive, emotional, aesthetic, imaginary, social, interpersonal or cultural matters. I also have less resources at my disposal for non-material cultural and personal development. In the *Explorations* section of this workbook, we take time to explore the "Uses of Nothing" and develop a fuller awareness of the immense riches of human personality, spirituality and social contacts apart from the creation and ownership of physical objects.

In advocating simplicity, I am not suggesting that we become as one-sidedly inner-directed as many people have become one-sidedly outer-directed. Duane Elgin has eloquently, and I think appropriately, argued that voluntary simplicity is about an elegant *balance* between inner and outer development and activity. I would take this point a little further and say that voluntary simplicity is about *integrated and wholistic* development of all aspects of our personhood, our relations with others and with the ecosphere. Modern industrial societies adopt an "either-or" approach to development and have stressed technical and scientific mastery over the physical systems of nature in order to meet the physical needs of humans (and artificial wants based on those needs) almost to the total exclusion of the development of the depth dimension of our lives.

Predictably, this has given us a society of immense material wealth and technical power at the price of spiritual, emotional and cultural poverty. Simple living merely offers a pathway to begin bringing these two aspects of our existence into greater harmony and proportion.

Coming to some measure of this awareness is sometimes an involuntary "accomplishment" as was the case for me. Shortly following the end of a seventeen-year marriage, I was alone with two children, my income slashed in half, one hide-a-bed, one pole lamp, a box of garage sale kitchen utensils and a total bank balance of $4.57. I remember my lawyer saying in his characteristically understated way, "You appear to be financially exposed." To say the least!

Life presented no immediate prospect of this situation improving or changing significantly. Concentrating on "getting ahead" in the traditional sense of that term would only have been frustrating. But it was a fine opportunity for shifting perspective to some of the qualitative aspects of living.

One summer morning, I had just finished a five-kilometre run and was strolling along to cool off. The air was mine, the sun was mine, and all the delicate colors and scents of summer seemed to be mine. It seemed to me that all the homeowners diligently working in their yards were beautifying the city specifically for me. It was like having hundreds of people working on the grounds of my own estate, cleaning it, tilling it and caring for it! Even the plants and animals that crowded everywhere in wonderful profusion seemed to give me themselves in some inalienable way that no divorce proceeding could threaten or disturb. In an objective sense, I had nothing. In a subjective sense, I felt as though I had everything and I needed nothing more. It was wonderful to realize that this plenitude of life had *always* been there and would always be there if only I took the time to attend to it and claim it.

Living simply also implies that the *means of meeting a given human need are proportionate to and appropriate for the need in question.* Understanding this concept must again take us into the realm of knowing the difference between needs and wants. But it also requires clear knowledge of *how* needs of different kinds are most appropriately met. Nutritious food in healthy quantities is the appropriate and proportionate means for fulfilling the human need to eat. Over-consumption of highly refined and unhealthy foods is neither a proportionate nor appropriate way to relieve anxiety or deal with depression. Computers are an appropriate and highly efficient means for handling symbolic information, solving certain problems and carrying on certain forms of communication. Virtual reality is neither a proportionate nor appropriate way of meeting social needs because the "reality" it presents is ersatz. Simple living grows from a commitment to always grow in consciousness, awareness and mindfulness of what it is we need, what it is we want, and what are the most appropriate, proportionate and ethical means of meeting our needs and fulfilling our wants. To a very considerable extent, market economies thrive by continually confusing and blurring these distinctions and by making implicit or explicit claims for products or services that try to meet needs with inappropriate means.

Simplicity, then, is *a decision to live more deeply.* In living simply, we choose to shift our attention and effort toward a more wholistic, balanced, integrated, proportionate and appropriate pattern of living. This new pattern honors both the inner, non-material, aesthetic and spiritual aspects of our lives as well as their material and physical aspects. We attend to what we wear, where we live, and how we move about in the world, but also we attend to what we say, the directness of our gaze, the singleness of our purposes in choosing our involvements and making our commitments.

The technology of being

The culture of consumerism requires a technology oriented toward having more. This technology manipulates *the outside world* in order to get more *things* from it. Consumerism teaches that these things then become the means to happiness. If the promise is unfulfilled, consumerism never suggests that its basic assumptions are out of line. It merely shifts our attention to some new or different thing. If we are not yet happy, content, peaceful, it is because we haven't yet found the correct thing that will deliver these experiences. Since we expect our well-being to come to us from a source outside ourselves (the products and services of the consumer culture), we are radically disempowered and made dependent for our sense of well-being.

Voluntary simplicity requires a different kind of technology that is oriented toward helping people *be* more. Simplicity returns responsibility for feelings of well-being to the individual, at least in part. As we have said above, voluntary simplicity is not an idealistic, but rather a practical philosophy. There are indeed certain *things* we must have to support personal health. But simplicity teaches that the means to well-being must be appropriate to what we need. Consumption of material things and services is essential for meeting basic survival needs, but consumption is inherently limited in the contribution it can make to certain kinds of personal and social development. Therefore, one focus of the technology of simplicity is the unity of self and universe, not the illusion that the two are separate, different and that therefore some separate "I" must have "that" in order to be whole.

When I was a boy of eleven or twelve, I used to go deer hunting with my father. He would waken me before dawn in the cold, crisp days of October and we would dress silently in the dim glow of a single night-light, not wanting to awaken the rest of the house. He had already packed his hunting gear in the car and we would slip out of the house and then go to an all-night truck stop restaurant for breakfast. It was still dark when we made our way into the woods by paths only my father seemed to know until we found the blind we had built days before, which overlooked pathways frequented by white-tailed deer. At first, I took no gun or bow and arrows, for I was too young. But later, I would sit alone in my own blind with my weapons ready while my father went to a different part of the woods.

The technique was called "still hunting." One simply sits silent, motionless and endlessly patient, waiting for deer to come along the paths. There was always an abundance of less patient hunters in the woods noisily crashing about making sure that the deer were more or less constantly on the move during the hunting season. Once in the blind, we would sit utterly still, our only movements being to breathe and to slowly turn our heads this way and that, scanning the bush for those enigmatic forms that seemed almost magically to appear out of nothing. We would sit this way for hours. At noon, we would take a break and return to the car for sandwiches and apples and discussion about where the deer might be if we had seen none that morning, or whether my father should or should not have taken a shot, given the distance, angle, brush cover and so forth concealing a deer we may have seen. On many days, especially archery hunting, success was getting a shot, much less getting a deer. On most days, "hunting" was sitting, interminably.

Now one might think that such activity would be boring. But as a youngster, my father taught me to overcome my boredom and impatience, the discomfort of sitting, and the disappointment of not seeing *deer* through the practice of continually renewed vigilance. Deer themselves were so elusive, so well-camouflaged and so silent that at any time one might "appear" that previously had been invisible but had been there all along. The possibility of a hidden deer created such motivation for me that moments of inattention or boredom were quickly dispensed in the renewed effort to discern the indiscernible. And every once in a while, this effort would succeed, which was reward enough to try even harder next time to stay still, silent and attentive. Twenty-five years later I would realize that what my father was teaching me, even though he didn't know it himself, was not hunting but *meditation*. Or more accurately, hunting became a pathway into meditation.

As my capacity for sitting still became more fully developed, something else happened. I could spend whole mornings in the bush from false dawn to noon, my senses rivetted on the changing patterns of light, color, form and sound in the forest. I learned to hear things wake up. I learned to see the forest at play, feeding, breathing. I sensed how the whole forest was a community that could listen to and observe me. If I was silent enough, it seemed to forget me, or perhaps accept me as part of itself, and then go about its business. Birds called, chipmunks played in the leaves, squirrels gathered hazelnuts, chickadees performed their bizarre acrobatic stunts searching for insect larvae. In all of this, I began to feel not like a hunter invading the bush for something I wanted from it, but like a part of the forest itself. I started to feel at home. I began to resent the occasional noisy intrusions of other hunters. At times, I felt a contentment so deep that it seemed I was absorbed in a timeless dream, dreaming the forest's dream of itself. As this capacity developed in me, I ceased to care whether or not I saw deer and I largely lost my desire to kill one. It was enough just to *be* in the bush and to be *with* the bush. It also became entirely irrelevant how I was dressed (other than needing protection from the elements) and whether or not I had a weapon. Eventually, I started to think of my bow and arrows, my hunting camouflage and boots, not as *hunting* gear for killing game, but as *camouflage gear* to hide from other hunters. They all would think I was out there to get my buck! They would think I was one of them. But in fact, I only *appeared* to be one of them. Once in the forest, little did they know, my main goal was just to sit!

This transformation from a fidgety twelve-year-old to a contemplative adolescent is an example of the applied technology of simplicity. *No thing* was required for this very rich experiential transformation in my capacities to see, hear and feel the forest. Hunting was an excuse, albeit a rationale both my father and I believed in, for something much more important to be taught and learned. I would not have needed to be hunting to learn this. In fact, I didn't need any *thing* that the consumer culture could provide. What was needful was the example of my father's wisdom, his love of the outdoors, his patience and generous sharing of this experience with me. But when I compare the meaning this experience has had for me and the further pathways to other meanings it has opened in my life to anything that I have ever owned in a material sense, the calculus of value is very easy to make. In a sense, my father gave me no thing but he helped me discover how to *be* more, here, now.

In exploring some of the *reasons* why a person might adopt simple living, we discussed the "know why" of voluntary simplicity. But the technology of voluntary simplicity is its "know how." This technology does not begin with discarding personal possessions and then searching for alternative, simpler ways of meeting the same needs. Rather, the technology begins with the *cultivation of mindfulness*. As we grow in our capacity for and enjoyment of mindfulness, then the outer aspects of our lives eventually and progressively come into alignment with this changed consciousness. Once the soil of mindfulness has been prepared within the person, then it can receive the seeds of suggestions from those who have experimented and learned how to meet basic and developmental needs more and more directly and simply so as to maintain mindfulness.

Mindfulness refers to a mental/emotional/physical state of attentive, wakeful awareness. It is the psychological dimension of a way of life of which voluntary simplicity is the physical dimension. Simplicity and mindfulness are *co-requisites* of each other. Simplicity feeds mindfulness, which feeds further simplicity. Those practitioners of simplicity who have attained the greatest purity of expression in simple living have also usually been the people who have manifested the highest degree of conscious mindfulness in their living. As mindfulness grows, we feel naturally inclined to clear away distracting complications from our lives and focus more intently on the tasks, commitments and activities that most naturally absorb our attention. As the clutter of our lives is gradually cleared away, there are fewer and fewer distractions from those activities and objects that are the focus of our mindful awareness. Hence, mindful awareness grows.

Developing mindfulness is not particularly complicated. It is a mental skill like memorization or problem-solving. It develops slowly over time and seldom appears as a sudden "Aha!," although many experiences of sudden insight are sprinkled along the path of growing mindfulness. If there is anything challenging about the cultivation of mindfulness it is the need for *patience* because the growth of mindfulness is very gradual; the need for *belief and persistence* because day-to-day progress is unnoticeable; the need for great *gentleness and self-forgiveness* because growth in mindfulness is marked by many false starts, backslides and gropings about; and the need for *discipline* in maintaining one's practice even when it seems that something so simple and so routine could never deliver what it promises.

In his utopian novel *Island*, Aldous Huxley imagined a tropical paradise he called Pala. Among many other interesting social innovations, the architects of Palanese society trained thousands of mina birds to call "Attention! Attention!" and "Here and now boys!" The birds helped remind the Palanese to sustain mindfulness at all times by paying attention to whatever was happening for them in the moment. Developing mindfulness begins precisely with this process of attentive awareness of the moment and the riches of experience each moment offers.

Practising such attentiveness naturally requires that we slow down the pace of our activities because we are seeking to become more deeply and intensely aware of each moment rather than hurrying from one moment to the next. Development of this kind of attentive consciousness naturally leads toward greater simplicity of living because mindful concentration of awareness simply leaves no room for *many* things. Few are sufficient because the few we have are so richly experienced.

I once watched a friend preparing a vegetable salad. She concentrated very closely on each step of the preparation process, examining the lettuce leaves one at a time as she washed them, watching the water rinse over the leaves and glitter and reflect in the sunlight of her kitchen. She dried and blotted the leaves, gently feeling each leaf through the moist texture of the towel she used. Next, she washed a sweet red pepper, then carefully dissected its seeds, weighing the knife in her hand, slicing with almost surgical attention to her movements, watching the light red juice of pepper stain the knife blade as she sliced the fruit to include it in the salad. Item by item, she proceeded this way, washing, feeling, smelling, breaking and cutting, placing and mixing the various parts of the various living things that would become our meal. Our conversation during this time was measured, thoughtful, and relaxed. I was as absorbed in watching her as she was in the preparation. My total experience of this particular salad was very different from the way we have been taught to perform such tasks.

In the preceding pages I have been careful not to call North American society "materialistic" but rather, *consumptive*. We have engineered a way of life that equates satisfaction with "through-put," an awkward but descriptive term related to the rate and quantity of things used up rather than the depth or intensity of experience. A truly materialistic society would love material things, which in turn would imply their conservation and enjoyment. My friend was being very materialistic in her enjoyment of making a salad which, paradoxically from our traditional point of view, is also a very *spiritual* attitude.

But a consumptive society is neither materialistic nor spiritual. It enjoys less and less as it tries to consume more and more. The very rate at which this process moves along virtually assures that it will not be an attentive and mindful process. As the rate of consumption goes ever higher and the level of attention drops ever lower, the general trend is toward greater and greater *unconsciousness*. We don't know what we are doing because we aren't paying attention, either to the sources of the things we use, the effects of making and harvesting them, the experience of using and enjoying them, or the consequences of having used them. What the consumptive society produces is stupor and waste rather than pleasure and well-made material artifacts. This is quite at variance with what it promises to deliver.

Another good example of what I mean by mindfulness can be found in any normal toddler. When my own children were experiencing their first few Christmas holidays, I saw a very clear example of how we teach ourselves to forsake mindfulness for consumptiveness. When they emerged from their beds on Christmas morning they met the traditional tree with piles of presents underneath. Being the only grandchildren in the family at the time, the haul was quite enormous. Each received a present and was taught how to open it, a skill that required right away that they forego their obvious delight with the wrapping paper, the soft ribbons, the dangley decorations affixed to the packages. Discovering the first toy of the season, both children settled down to play and thoroughly explore the possibilities of these new objects. This would have taken all morning, as it should. But gathered all around were adult relatives whose joy in the season had come to mean experiencing abundance-as-quantity rather than abundance-as-richness. The object of this Christmas morning exercise was to *open* presents, not particularly to experience them. It was necessary to get on with the next thing, to stay in motion, to consume. So, not without smiles or gentleness, one present after another was taken away to be replaced by an unopened package. I remember at one point the expression of bewilderment on my son's face as he was trying to "get" the meaning of this behavior. Being a child, he learned very quickly. By late morning, opening presents had turned into the pandemonium of ripping paper, which the adults had subtly communicated was their expectation. By lunchtime, all the presents were open, the new toys in various corners of the family room and my children off playing with the empty boxes and none of the toys. They had learned well. Life in the consumer society is the moment of newness, the adrenal push of discovery, the hypercharged, narcotic-like flash of novelty that goes with "through-put." Thou shalt not pay attention. Thou shalt not linger. Thou shalt not enjoy. Thou shalt keep moving.

In relating this anecdote, I do not disparage the intentions of my family in wanting to give to my children abundantly. I only point out a rather self-defeating illusion to which we are all prone. The real poverty of our generation is that we don't know how to savor as well as we know how to consume. The capacity for mindful absorption in life is often something we must relearn from our children.

Thus, the development of mindfulness includes adopting not a childish, but a child-like approach to our experience. It is patient, receptive, open, non-judgmental, intensely absorbed in the moment. And this general attitude, in the more developed forms of mindful awareness, is carried into *every* act of daily life: eating, walking, sitting, working, bathing, love-making, conversing, touching, waiting, playing, thinking, feeling.

Implicit in all of this is the fact that the technology of simple living is not an exterior or mechanical technology, but an inner and personal one. Mindfulness is developed as much as an attitude of the *body* as it is of the mind. Perhaps more so. The hallmark of a technical civilization oriented toward consumerism has been an intellectualization of education and a distancing of consciousness from any grounding in sensory experience. Information is transferred in visual media by increasingly impersonal means.

But when we consider the practices that help develop mindfulness, they often begin with or include physical and emotional disciplines as well as mental work. Meditation itself depends very much on postural forms and breathing disciplines that change the focal length of conscious awareness. Dance, martial arts, the fine arts such as painting, sculpture and music, all require physical involvement as an integral part of developing mental attention. It seems that we come to the "knowledge" of what mindfulness is as much by intuitive absorption as by conscious teaching.

This point reflects back on what I said earlier when I identified mindfulness and simple living as *co-requisites* of each other. Neither mindfulness nor simplicity are patterns of being that I can come to simply by changing my intellectual opinions or learning a concept of some sort. The content of the mindful experience of simple living is not concepts or opinions. It is something we *become*, not something we *think*. Until we become it in some measure— that is, actually do it—we don't understand it either.

There are many excellent resources for developing greater mindfulness and I have listed some of them in the recommended reading section of this book. It isn't my purpose here to reiterate what has been done so well by so many others over the last four thousand years. But the section on *Explorations* that follows is intended to help us become more mindful and more aware of how we presently pattern our lives and to continually repeat that we *do* have choice in the matter of how we will live. Necessarily, because this is a book, our explorations must be confined more or less to the realm of ideas and concepts. I have just argued that this is not enough to develop mindfulness and this book, by itself, will not be effective in helping you develop mindfulness. I hope, however, that it will help with a process a great Latin American popular educator, Paulo Freire, termed "conscientization:" the gradual process of bringing into conscious awareness our overall social and personal predicament so that change becomes possible. No change is possible when we are *unconscious* of our predicament. Completing the explorations exercises will not establish you in a life of mindful simplicity, but I hope the exercises will help carry you toward the point where you begin to behave in ways that develop both.

2
Explorations

Explorations

This part of *Simplicity* consists of exercises to help clarify personal values and open new perspectives on simple living and its alternatives. Some explorations will ask you to describe different aspects of your present way of life. Others will invite you to imagine new possibilities for yourself and your family. Take time during your explorations and write thoughtful responses. You may be surprised at what you discover.

Obtain some paper and a pen, or better yet, set up a special notebook with looseleaf paper to record your explorations. Think of it as a kind of travel diary in which you keep notes, insights, and accounts of feelings and intuitions as you survey each new bit of terrain. You may find that you want to repeat exercises over a considerable period of time and that this process of looking back and then forward contains within itself much energy for further growth in awareness.

Here and now[7]

When an artist begins a new work, she gathers fresh canvas or paper, fresh paints or crayons, and sets aside the work just completed. When a writer begins a new story, he first finds some fresh paper and perhaps a new pen, or these days, may insert a new diskette in the computer and open a new file! When we want to learn a new dance, we push back the furniture to create an open space for this new activity and we clear a space on our calendar for dance lessons.

In the following exercise, we will be clearing a mental/emotional/spiritual "space" to allow room for further explorations. We do this by characterizing and describing our present situation. We say whatever there is to say about it in order to describe this present moment in our lives, our "situation as a whole" with its problems, rewards, tensions and contentments. We do this not in order to solve problems or arrive at grand insights so much as to slow down and give ourselves the gift of a methodical, systematic self-examination. We do not rate our progress. We do not judge our "successes" or "failures" or try to discern big "patterns." The objective of this exercise is simply to increase a little bit our *awareness* of the totality of our life situation here and now.

To assist with this process, I offer some "stem" questions or prompts that relate to different aspects of living. Consider each area in turn. Don't try to write an exhaustive description of each life area but rather make a few pithy notes that capture the essence of what is or isn't happening in that area of your life. Since your notes will be entirely private, you can be completely honest with yourself.

Anything you write is acceptable. Judging yourself, editing or omitting things only leaves furniture on the dance floor!

1. *Think about this present time in your life as a whole. Write a paragraph or sketch a picture that describes this time in your life.*

2. *How would you describe the feelings that have most characterized this time?*

3. *Describe the work you do, its rewards, frustrations, opportunities and limitations.*

4. *Describe your current financial situation with particular attention to its emotional implications for you.*

5. *Name and briefly describe the relationships in your life that have a major impact on you, both positive and negative.*

6. *Describe how you have felt physically, your overall level of health or illness, your sexual well-being or lack of it, your energy level, and any particularly noteworthy experiences of physical pleasure or pain or injury.*

7. *Describe your experience of community or of the world of social and interpersonal contacts beyond the close relationships that you described above.*

8. *Describe your spirituality. How do you experience spirituality at this point in your life and how do you attempt to live it?*

9. *How would you describe the major problem areas of your life? In what areas do you feel the most need for growth, healing or development?*

10. In what areas of your life do you experience the most vitality, strength and reward? Where are your "power surges" coming from?

11. Draw a picture or create a symbol that you feel expresses this time as a whole. Alternatively, you may wish to create a poem, a song, an artwork or a ceremony/ritual that expresses this time and that you can perform or create at an appropriate time and place.

[This exercise is an adaptation of the "Period Log" exercise developed by Ira Progoff for the National Intensive Journal Program. See references.]

The best things in life...

What is life for anyway? The answer to this question may be very different for different people. For some, it may be based on the feelings of pleasure they derive from various activities, from relationships or from achievements. For others, the purpose of life may be related to religious faith, spiritual beliefs, a calling or craft or trade. Others may want to make a contribution of some kind to our society or culture, or perhaps they find the purpose of their lives in caring for family members, children or friends.

Voluntary simplicity assumes that we will find greatest satisfaction and reward in life when our daily round of activities grows out of the purposes and goals we believe are most important. Experiences of great pleasure and deep meaning are often themselves the signposts to what we value and what is best for us. A simple life is one in which we focus our energies on the things we know are best for us. Often, however, the pace of modern life leaves us little time to remember or re-centre our activities on the "best things in life."

In the following exploration, we begin by recalling some past experiences of great satisfaction, joy and reward. Then we relate these experiences to aspects of "material culture," and finally to our present daily round of activities.

To prepare for this exploration, it will be helpful to explain the difference between "material culture" and "non-material culture."

Material culture refers to physical objects produced by human activities or collected by human beings from the environment. Examples include cars, stereos, boats and houses.

Non-material culture refers to creations of human beings that are essentially invisible or non-material. In some cases, an object or thing may be used to reproduce or elaborate the non-material artifact, but is not essential to its nature. Examples of non-material culture are language, stories, dramas, legends, philosophies, scientific theories, songs, etc. We may use amplifiers and recording devices to *store and transmit* songs, but such devices are not essential to the creation of music. In general, when a people dies so does its non-material culture unless it has been recorded in some fashion. Its material culture may remain as the ruins of buildings, artworks, tools and so on.

1. List as many examples as you can of <u>material</u> culture.

2. Now list as many examples as you can of <u>non-material</u> culture.

3. Compare your lists of material and non-material cultural items. Which list is longer? What does this difference suggest to you?

4. What opportunities do you think the difference in the two lists might represent?

5. How do you relate the length of these two different lists to the ideas of development and civilization? Be honest.

Now relax and let your mind drift back over your entire life up to this time. Write a paragraph describing each of three "high points" in your life. These are times when you experienced great joy, vitality and satisfaction in being alive. Then answer the following questions after writing each account.

1. What were you doing?

2. Who were you with?

3. What aspects of this time/experience brought you most fulfilment?

4. Were there articles of material culture essential to making this experience possible? If so, what were they?

5. What, if anything, prevents you from repeating this experience or others like it?

Logging the daily round

Much of what we do much of the time is more or less unconscious. That is, many of our activities are driven by habit or what we think is necessity. We don't think much about what we do. We spend lots of time "going through the motions." Since much of our social activity requires interacting with machines that operate on repetitive cycles, our activities can become even more automatic. Many people spend a considerable period in the car, and for experienced drivers, driving is an almost automatic behavior. We are conscious, of course, but not *mindful* of what we are doing.

Voluntary simplicity assumes that activities that are entered into with mindfulness—that is, with full attention to the voluntariness of our actions—are more rewarding and pleasurable than habit-driven or semi-conscious routines.

When I have done time management workshops, I've often asked participants to record how they spend their time on a "typical" day, or during the last week. Often people have a hard time remembering what they did. Sometimes their memories are even distorted by how they wish they had spent the time!

To escape the delusions of wishful thinking and to move another step in our mindfulness of how we are living, it is helpful to prepare a log record of our daily round. Like a ship's log, this is a diary-like record of what we do all day. To prepare for the next exploration, I suggest that you keep a log of your daily activities for at least one week.

I have heard people say that they have no "typical" days or weeks. Their activities are always changing. That's fine.

Record whatever it is you do for one week. There will still be many themes that carry over from one week to the next.

Set aside seven pages of your notebook and log all of your activities for the next seven days, hour by hour. If you have an electronic watch with a built-in alarm, it might be helpful to set your watch to prompt you to log your activities, say, at lunch time (for the morning hours), at supper time (for the afternoon hours), and just before bed (for the evening hours). Log __everything__ no matter how personal or trivial it may seem. Your log is for your eyes only. Make no judgments and don't censor your entries. For one week, you are an "anthropologist" studying the wonderful and peculiar behaviors of an exotic culture in the activities of one of its members. Enjoy yourself!

Having completed your daily round log for a week, now review your entries and ask some questions about them. Be gentle with yourself in all your questions. All of us drift into patterns of behavior that are sometimes out of harmony with our intentions and desires. The purpose of this exploration is growth in mindfulness, that is to become more aware of what in fact we are doing with our time and energy so that new choices become possible if we want them.

1. *Review the activities you have logged. How many of them bring the kind of reward and sense of satisfaction that you associate with the "peak experiences" of your life?*

2. *If some activities are not rewarding or satisfying, what are they for? Are they necessary or could they be changed, reorganized or eliminated?*

DAILY ROUND	
TIME	ACTIVITIES

3. To what extent is your daily round of activity focused on aspects of material culture? What rewards does this bring into your life?

4. To what extent does your daily activity help achieve your goals in life? Is it achieving someone else's goals? If so, whose? Do you endorse these goals?

5. Design for yourself a daily round of activities that would bring you closer to doing more of the things you find most rewarding and important in life. When you have completed your design for an ideal daily round, discuss what this review has meant to you with a close friend, partner or family member.

The uses of nothing

Daily living in a consumption-oriented society finds us with a barrage of advertising messages and subtle social pressures that equate consumption with well-being. Over a lifetime, this process can undermine confidence in our intrinsic powers as human beings to experience pleasure and meaning in life apart from consuming, owning and possessing. We come to believe that what we *are* is defined by what we *have*. Perhaps we come to think that our experience of being human is provided by the things we own.

In this exercise, we take time to recognize our own intrinsic power as human beings. That is, we remember the capacities that are ours apart from the things we own or consume.

Imagine that you are on a tropical island far from "civilization." You have no tools or other possessions except for your clothing. There is ample fresh water to drink, plenty of vegetable foods for the picking and the climate requires no clothing or special shelter. The island is densely inhabited with plants and animals but none of these present any real danger to human beings.

1. *Take a few minutes and list as many activities as you can think of that you could pursue as an individual. Then rate the reward value of each activity on a scale from one (slightly rewarding) to 10 (extremely rewarding).*

2. *Next, imagine you are part of a group on this island and make another list of all the activities that would be possible in relationship with other people. You can discuss this exercise with friends or members of your family to generate more ideas. Now review your list and rate the reward value of each activity on a scale from 1 (slightly rewarding) to 10 (very rewarding).*

3. *Describe the environmental impacts of your top three activities.*

4. *Now repeat this exercise, assuming that you can bring with you to the island anything that could be purchased for $100 or less.*

   What would you purchase?

   How many activities will it add to your list? Be specific.

   What effect do these additional activities have on the island environment?

What effect do these additional activities have on your social life with the other islanders? Have they strengthened bonds between you and enriched your community or not?

5. *Repeat the exercise again, this time assuming that you have $10,000 to spend.*

   What would you buy?

   How many additional activity choices does it open to you and how would you rate these options compared to those on your first list?

6. *Review your feelings and record the results of these exercises.*

7. *What does society tell you about the relation between money, consumption, ownership and well-being?*

8. *How does this actually square with your experience of life?*

9. *What were the relative environmental consequences of lists 1, 2 and 3?*

10. *Were the differences in environmental impact worth the difference in reward value, even from a purely human point of view?*

I want it now!

The products and services we *need* are those things without which we either could not survive physically or the lack of which would so diminish the scope of our lives that we could not develop our full human potential. Clearly, some needs are basic to all human beings, such as the need for food and water. Other needs are basic to all people living in certain regions, such as the need for heated shelters in northern climates. Some needs such as those for love, social esteem and meaningful work may not be directly related to physical survival, but they are necessary to emotional and psychological development and well-being.

The psychologist Abraham Maslow[8] suggested that human needs could be arranged in a hierarchy or pyramid with basic needs like food and shelter at the bottom, social and self-esteem needs occupying a middle layer, and "self-actualization" or spiritual needs standing at the top of the hierarchy. In arranging needs in this way, Maslow didn't mean that spiritual or self-actualization needs were more important than basic physical needs. On the contrary, personal and spiritual development rested on the satisfaction of basic needs for its *foundation.* Maslow believed that there was little point in trying to develop the actualization potentials of the human spirit when basic needs were unmet or insecure. In this, he had much in common with the world's spiritual teachers who have seldom recommended preaching liberation or holiness to the starving!

Products and services we *want* usually relate to items that go far beyond essential human needs. We need transportation, but a luxuriously appointed sports car for personal use has clearly moved into the realm of things we might want. One of the ways a modern, market-oriented economy maintains its growth momentum is to use advertising and market promotion strategies to confuse wants and needs, or at least to *associate* them so closely that over a long period of time, they wind up being confused. It has often been observed how the marketing of automobiles has moved away from meeting the basic human need for transportation and has been based instead on associations to the human impulses for sexual gratification, acquiring or displaying social status, exercising power and expressing dominance over others (as in auto racing) or over our environment (the all-terrain vehicle phenomenon).

Meeting basic needs is essential to our health and well-being. Meeting actualization needs is essential to the full flowering of our humanity. Voluntary simplicity aims to meet both sets of needs as *directly* and *simply* as possible. In the following exploration, we will be examining our needs and how we are currently trying to meet them, how successful these efforts are and what alternatives we might imagine.

Open a new section in your notebook for this exercise. Divide the first page of your new section in half from top to bottom. On the left side of the page, list as many examples as you can of what you think are the needs essential to human health and physical survival. On the right side of the page, list those things that you think are essential to the development of what you consider to be a fully human person. Now, beginning on a fresh page, copy one need at the top of the page and answer the questions that follow on the balance of the page. Add pages if you wish. Continue until you have explored all needs on both of your lists.

1. *How can this need be met most directly?*

2. *How are you meeting this need in your life right now or what do you think would meet this need?*

3. *Name as many environmental, social, economic and spiritual consequences as you can of the way you are now meeting this need.*

4. *Either alone or in discussion with others, devise as many alternative ways of meeting this need as you can think of that would either be more direct, simpler or reduce the negative environmental and other impacts of your current way of meeting this need.*

Now set aside your worksheets and consider goods or services which are clearly in the category of wants. On a fresh page of your workbook, list some examples of wants from your own life.

In your notebook, set up a separate sheet for each want and answer the following questions for each one:

1. *If needs are a basic "fact of life" for human beings, where did this want come from?*

2. *How did you develop this want?*

3. *What exactly do you hope to experience if you acquire it?*

4. *What do you predict will be the environmental, economic, social, spiritual and personal consequences, both positive and negative, of acquiring the thing you want?*

5. *By means of what activities had you planned to pursue the fulfilment of this want, and using how much time?*

7. *Are there ways of satisfying this aspiration that have less environmental, social, economic, spiritual, etc., impact? If so, how?*

8. *Describe one occasion when you fulfilled a want and one time when you fulfilled a need. Do the same limits apply to each kind of experience?*

9. *If needs are limited by our natural capacities for fulfilment but wants are not, what does this imply for the environment and the ability of others to meet their needs in the future?*

10. *What life changes, if any, do you feel you want to make in light of this exercise?*

My planet for a cup of coffee

One fertile area for the growth of mindfulness of our way of life is to reflect on the things we buy and use. Much of the time, we purchase machines, products and services because they help us meet a need of some sort, but we don't think much about how this particular product came to be as it is, where it came from, whether it meets the need we feel or whether, perhaps, it goes far beyond what we need or even want. It is helpful, for example, to ask ourselves whether we really want to pay the price of products and services that are designed for a vast array of individual tastes and preferences and are therefore highly marketable from a corporate perspective, but that might represent excessive costs to almost all individual users of the product or service. Is it appropriate, for example, for those who want reliable basic telephone service to subsidize the cost of call waiting, call trace, call display, call forwarding and data transfer services for the minority of people who want these services?

In the following exploration, we will be thinking about the meaning of material progress, diminishing returns, and the consequences of focusing so much creative effort on generating economic profit. We will be weighing the value of invention and technical developments in material culture in terms of the *needs they meet* rather than the profits they can turn.

I met Quinn, hermit and storyteller extraordinaire, living in the backwoods of Northern Ontario in the early '80s. He ranted about many things, but one morning he got going about his cup of coffee.

"Know what coffee costs ya these days?," he fumed. "Arm and half o' leg, that's what!"

"And how's that?" I asked.

"Well," he began, "when my pappy came into these parts, he made 'camp coffee.' That's where ya just dump some coffee into a pan o' boilin' water and let 'er brew. Then ya take 'er off the heat, drip in some cold water to settle the grounds and have yer brew.

"Well, pappy kept gettin' grounds in his cup. So he took a sock and put the grounds in his sock and soaked it like a tea bag in the boilin' water and that gave coffee too, only better, 'cause it had no grounds.

"Later then, they came up with them metal pots with

the little basket for the grounds and the glass bubble on top so ya could tell how dark yer coffee was gettin'. All in all, it tasted better than socks! So coffee was a little better.

"Now one day, they drove hydro in here and ya could put yer coffee pot on an electric stove and heat it that way instead o' on the woodstove. That didn't make the coffee any better a'tall, but I guess the electric stove was good fer some other stuff, so it sorta made sense.

"Then somebody decided 'tweren't good enough to make yer coffee on the stove and ya better have a different gizmo fer it. So they come up with them plug-in coffee pots that like had their own little stove right inside 'em, 'cept you couldn't use 'em for nothin' else but coffee. They made a bundle on them, they did!

"Well, once they got people into buyin' them things, they got them computer chips and all. Now ya can get a coffee pot with brains yet! It's got programs and dials and settin's and needs to have its innards flushed out every week just like a fastin' yogi. It'll make coffee even if ya ain't there! Makes the same coffee as pappy's sock, 'cept pappy's sock was free and these gizmos cost ya a hundred bucks. They call that progress."

1. *Select one item of material culture within your home that has undergone considerable "development" since it was first introduced, e.g. refrigerator, knife, washing machine. In your notebook, identify the need this item was intended to fulfil.*

2. *Trace the stages of development of this device over the years. If you don't know what they are, it is interesting to do some reading on how common items of our material culture have been developed. Summarize this process briefly in your notebook.*

3. Can you identify any point in the development of this device, service or item where changes in the device no longer produced improvements in its function or intended use? If so, when?

4. What were the results of the extra changes?

5. Who benefited most from these changes?

6. At any point, do you think "development" became <u>overdevelopment</u>? If so, where?

7. What relation exists between this device and the need it is intended to fulfil at the end of its course of development compared to the beginning?

8. What does this approach to development cost each of us in terms of time, money, the environment, aesthetic quality of life, spiritual peace, international and intercultural understanding and harmony?

9. What alternatives to this sort of system can you imagine?

10. What steps are you willing to take to move toward such alternatives?

To my children's children's children

Another aspect of the development of mindfulness is the awareness that we are part of a long flow of historical events. The human story up to this time has brought us to where we are in the development of our society and of our personal consciousness. Our actions, our lives, will contribute to the flow of events that sets the stage for future generations. One principle of "sustainable development" has been *intergenerational equity*. This principle is the recognition that future generations will feel the consequences of our decisions and we should take their interests into account. But intergenerational equity is an ethical concept that many of us find quite abstract. In the following exploration, we will be taking a guided fantasy journey into the future to experience the reality of intergenerational connections. After making this "thought experiment," we may discover that our lives contain emotional and spiritual bonds with the past and future that far exceed the bounds set by the logic of self-interest.

Find a place where you can be quiet and undisturbed for an hour or so. Sit in a relaxed and attentive position and take eight or 10 deep breaths to relax and become more centred.

Perhaps you have heard of a "time capsule," a container of documents and artifacts that is sealed up in a wall or stone slab to be opened at some future date. In the following exploration, you have the opportunity to prepare a document for such a time capsule, although in this case, the time capsule will be the property of your own family. Your task is to write a letter to your great-great-great-grandchild. It is helpful to actually visualize this child holding your letter as he or she stands somewhere in the 22nd century. This child is your own descendant, part of your family. This exploration is especially helpful to growth in mindfulness if you don't treat it as an "exercise" but as a real-life assignment. You can take steps to provide that your letter will actually be delivered.

The questions listed below are intended to help you focus your attention on issues central to this book but they are by no means exhaustive. The overarching concern is that you use this exploration as an opportunity to develop a sense of your intimate connection with future generations.

1. Describe to your descendant what the world was like for you at the end of the 20th century.

2. Describe what may have worried you about the future and what you did to assure the future for your descendants.

3. What were your concerns for the world that your descendants would inherit and how did you express those concerns?

4. What do you imagine the world of AD 2100 to be like?

5. Based on your experience of life in the 20th century, what would you pass along to your descendant by way of "sage advice" on how to live sustainably?

6. Now in your imagination, return to our time and the place you are in. What has writing this letter meant to you? What are you feeling and thinking about it?

Where the money goes

Most of us must purchase things in order to live if we live in modern, urbanized communities. How we deploy our financial resources and how we make purchasing decisions are major opportunities for developing more thoughtful and conscious approaches to consumption. Like many other aspects of our lives, how and what we spend our money on can become matters of routine. To the extent that our consumption decisions are habit-driven, we can waste money, resources and life-time without really appreciating what it costs us. We may also get "locked in" to purchasing behaviors that we might otherwise choose to change if we simply took the time to become more conscious of what we were doing and made decisions accordingly.

In the following exploration, you'll examine where your money actually goes. If you have no financial records or receipts available to provide this information, some of it can be recovered from banks, utility companies, credit vendors and the like. But if you haven't kept records, you might consider setting up a record-keeping system for six months or so. You can't make conscious, responsible decisions unless you have accurate, complete information.

As you consider how much money you have made and how you have disposed of it during the last year, consider also how much purchasing power you have used to either support the status quo or to foster change in society. You may be surprised at how much financial influence you actually do have, even though it may have been disposed of in small amounts in many directions.

Finally, you will be exploring how your purchasing decisions have affected your quality of life, whether they have been empowering or disempowering choices, and how your purchasing decisions might be reoriented to serve more satisfying goals.

Mini-budget review

1. What was your net income from all sources last year?
$_____

2. List some major expenditures for your household:

Rent/mortgage payments $_____
Hydro (electricity) $_____
Water/sewer services $_____
Gas/oil/coal (heating) $_____
Insurance $_____
Maintenance and repairs $_____

Car payments or upkeep $_____
Car insurance $_____
Fuel, oil and repairs $_____

Food (including meals out) $_____
Household supplies $_____
Clothing $_____
Laundry, dry cleaning, etc. $_____
Drugs, dental and medical devices $_____
Entertainment $_____
Gifts $_____
Vacation (holidays) & travel $_____

Lessons & educational fees $_____
Life insurance, disability coverage $_____
Retirement/educational savings $_____
Child-related (e.g. daycare) $_____
Investments $_____
Other savings $_____
Miscellaneous $_____

Major purchases during last 12 months:
Item: _____ $_____
_____ $_____
_____ $_____
_____ $_____
_____ $_____

Total expenditures: $_____

3. *Take some time and sift through receipts, credit card payment notices and other items of information to get a clear understanding of exactly how your income was spent in each of the lump sum categories listed above. As this picture becomes clearer for you, especially with regard to major purchasing decisions, consider the purchasing decision review questions proposed by the Simple Living Collective of San Francisco.[9]*

• *Does what I own or buy promote activity, self-reliance and involvement, or does it induce passivity and dependence?*

• *Are my consumption patterns basically satisfying, or do I buy much that serves no real need?*

• *How tied is my present job and lifestyle to instalment payments, maintenance and repair costs, and the expectations of others?*

• *Do I consider the impact of my consumption patterns on other people and on the Earth?*

4. *Note any insights you might have gained from applying these questions to your purchasing decisions of the last year.*

5. *Now for discovery purposes, make a budgeting plan that would allow you to live on 75% of your present income or make only 75% of your present expenditures.*

What changes would you have to make? Be specific. Try to devise a workable plan and think about the shifts in lifestyle that would be required. Consider both the "down side" and the "up side" of such changes. How could such changes represent opportunities?

6. Finally, repeat the above exercise, but this time make a plan to live on 50% of your present income.

What would you gain?

What would you lose?

What would be the opportunities in such a situation?

Which, if any, of these changes are you going to make?

Visioning a well world[10]

One of the most empowering discoveries we can make when we cultivate mindfulness and simple living is our individual power of imagination. The consumer culture runs on images. It entrains our imaginations to visions of the good life that have been fashioned by someone else. These images of the good life have two effects. One is to alienate us from the power of our own imagination, convincing us that we cannot imagine a world better than the one being offered to us by the corporate consumer culture. How often have we been promised experiences, benefits, or payoffs "beyond our wildest dreams?" This is as much as to say, "We, the manufacturers of this product sold by means of these fantasy images, have imagined the future even better than you could! Therefore, you should buy *our* vision of the good life."

The second effect of this process is that we tend to lose touch with and cease to believe in the value of our own visions as guiding stars for our living. This may mean that we begin trying to achieve goals in life that have come into us from outside, from someone else, and that serve someone else's purposes, rather than responding to images that spontaneously spring from within ourselves and express our own development needs. In the long run, this means that our life energy is spent achieving goals that belong to someone else but that we have let ourselves be convinced will really bring us satisfaction.

None of this is to say that we necessarily have to follow our own dreams, no matter what. There is room for dialogue with others, for "collective dreaming" where we can fashion visions that are shared by a group or a community. It is only to point out that very little dialogue based on equality and mutual respect characterizes the approach of industrial societies to the visioning process.

I have found visioning and imagination to be very important activities in my own life because I usually don't change either my habits or my values because of rational decisions based on facts. Rather, I fall in love with some inner image of what I want to experience or become. I am informed by facts, but I am *moved* by images.

As I have become more sensitive to this process in my own consciousness, I have also become more sensitized to how basic is the use of imagery (or rather *alienated* imagery) to advertising, marketing and consumptive living. One way of reducing our vulnerability to influence from these manipulative forces in our society is to moderate or eliminate our exposure to them, especially from television and radio. It is true that these media *can* be both entertaining and informative. But it's well worth the time to do an exercise similar to *Logging the Daily Round* to log our television viewing time and radio listening and then identify from all of those hours, how much education and entertainment was actually available to us and how much we retained. Even news programs and documentaries can be very light on education and heavy on commercialized "impression management" which is little more than current events advertising.

When we take the initiative to shut off the tap of imagery and suggestion flooding in from outside, there is a space of time during which nothing seems to be happening. This can be boring and it is then we are tempted to return to being "entertained." This "empty" space is merely evidence of how our own imaginative capacities have been lulled to sleep by media and a marketing culture. But soon, our own capacity for imaginative experience re-emerges.

In the following exploration, we reconnect with our own imaginative powers and also seek personal visions of a healthy world. We all carry within ourselves such an image of a well world. We have only to turn our attention in the right direction and take some time to discover it.

Find a place where you can be quiet and undisturbed for an hour or so. Sit in a relaxed and attentive position and take eight or 10 deep breaths to relax and become more centred.

Clear your mind of all the concerns of the day and take a short mental vacation. We are going to time-travel to your own community 30 years into the future. The people in this future time (and all those in between) have learned how to live in a healthy way. They have reshaped your community, neighborhood, city, village, so as to sustain this wellness and assure that all citizens enjoy it. You now walk about in this community and see all that they have achieved. You have this image within you at some level. It may be fragmentary, or it may be sounds or feelings rather than pictures. All of these are "images," so welcome whatever comes to you. Record a "travel log" of your visit to a future healthy world. To help with this process, I have included some questions for you to consider and log in your notebook:

1. *What does this community look like? Describe as much as you can.*

2. *What are people doing to earn a living?*

3. *What do people do for entertainment and recreation?*

4. *How have cities changed?*

5. *How do people live in the countryside?*

6. *How do people get from place to place in this world?*

7. *How does the landscape smell, look, sound?*

8. *Now you can see a family. What does the family of your well world look like? What are they doing and how do they live?*

9. *Go to a public place like a market or a park. How does this place look? How has it changed from similar places in your own time?*

10. *What have the people in your well world learned or what do they do that is most important to maintaining their own health and that of the planet/community?*

11. *What two steps do you want to take in your own life in the present time to help move a little bit in the direction of your well world vision?*

This exercise can also be done in a group setting. Group members can share their individual visions of a well world through verbal description, singing, drama, sculpture, etc.

After discussion, see if you can form a consensus on some goals for group action as well as individual action, or see if you can devise ways for the group to support each of its members as individuals to take action to bring change to their own situations.

[This exploration is based on visioning exercises developed by Dr. Trevor Hancock, a health consultant working in the Toronto-region with the Canadian Healthy Communities Project in partnership with the World Health Organization, the Canadian Public Health Association, and Health and Welfare Canada, 1987.]

Simplicity study circles

We have ample proof of the power of groups to support individual efforts at personal transformation. As soon as voluntary simplicity moves beyond being a subject of intellectual curiosity and into the realm of lived experience, group work can be a valuable pathway for personal change. It is tempting to minimize what is actually involved in the challenge of sustainable livelihood: nothing less than recovering from a very pervasive and deep-seated addiction. Like other addictions, our destructive relationship with consumerism has emotional, spiritual, intellectual and behavioral roots with a long history of development. Unlike other forms of addiction, consumerism has the patina of public acceptability. When we over-consume goods and services, we experience less social censure than if we over-consume alcohol, tobacco or opiates. This being the case, it is especially helpful to develop a community of people who share your own love of simplicity and dedication to sustainable livelihood.

The history of the development of Alcoholics Anonymous, and all of the subsequent "anonymous" groups that have followed the 12-step recovery program, suggests how important group work can be in increasing our awareness of self-destructive behaviors and establishing healthier patterns of living.

The Global Action Plan, headquartered in New York, promotes the formation of neighborhood-based action teams of eight to 12 people who commit themselves to environmental action at the household and personal level. Using the World Conservation Strategy as a guide, participants review eight different areas of their lifestyle (e.g. energy use, waste generation, etc.) and work together over a six-month period to change habits and behaviors that are ecologically destructive.

It is also frequently the case that personal change begins with some kind of conference, group workshop or study circle. When we join with others in groups to examine issues of importance to us, we benefit from their insights as well as our own. We avail ourselves of the creativity and life experience of other group members who might be able to help us see our own situation from a new angle.

The "technology" of mindfulness is highly developed within the major spiritual traditions of the world. The practice of solitary, celibate asceticism is well understood within monastic settings. But much still needs to be created in terms of living a joyful simplicity within family and community. Here we can see a special role for group work and group support on the journey to a simpler lifestyle. Groups can be rich, creative resources for their members and much of what we do, what we use, and how we are in the world needs to be re-created if we are to sustain human cultures in the future. Voluntary simplicity is a tremendous creative challenge, one that is ideally suited to working in community with others.

In this section, we will present some group activity plans that have the same general goal as the individual exploration exercises presented in the previous section. You may wish to establish a study circle on simplicity with your neighbors, members of your family, a church or community group, or a group of co-workers. Perhaps you will take a leadership role in such a group, or you may be the "sponsor/organizer" who enlists someone else to provide group leadership. In either case, the following exercises are offered as starting places for group discussions and learning experiences. Be willing to modify, innovate and depart from the suggested "agenda" if your work together calls for such changes. The general goal of all of these experiments is *to become more awake and mindful of our experience,* to learn *to live more lightly on planet Earth,* and to learn *to relate more fully and richly with others in pursuit of our highest values.* There will be many "right" ways to achieve these goals.

Study circles

The Topsfield Foundation of Pomfret, Connecticut, has established the Study Circle Resource Center, which publishes a variety of resource materials on conducting "study circles" on a variety of issues (see Recommended Reading section for specific references and address). A study circle is a group of 5-20 people who meet on several occasions to discuss critical social or personal issues. Meetings last about two hours and are facilitated by leaders who use a study circle group format. The overall goal of the groups is to deepen participants' understanding of an issue by focusing on the values that underlie opinions.

A typical study circle process would include intro- ductions of group members, review of study circle groundrules for participation, discussion of personal interest in or experience with an issue (in this case, voluntary simplicity), sharing a range of views on the subject, group discussion and deliberation, summary of the common ground found during the discussion, and finally, evaluation and next steps (which can include individual or group action on the issue). The Study Circle Resource Centre provides simple and well-written tips for group leaders, sponsor/organizers, and group participants. A study circle process is clearly one way of exploring voluntary simplicity in a group context.

Retreats and workshops

An alternative to study circles is to convene a retreat or a workshop on simplicity. A workshop might involve a single evening or Saturday afternoon, or might be planned as a multi-day event. A retreat usually involves a special residential situation where participants live at a retreat centre, camp or other facility designed for the purpose. Retreats and workshops are usually one-shot events. As such, they lack the continuity required for solid group support for changes to individual lifestyle. Nevertheless, a well-designed workshop can stimulate community interest in the issue at hand and challenge individuals to develop their understanding of simplicity and its application in their lives. Following the sample agendas for group activities, I have suggested some schedules for workshops of one evening, one day and two days' duration.

HERE AND NOW

(For groups)

Purpose: To create a space and time for participants to become aware, to acknowledge, and to fully express how they feel to be alive in the present; to ceremonialize their concerns for the planet, for each other, and for future generations; to clear a space for new work.

Time required: About two hours for a group of eight people.

Materials and equipment: Pens and notebooks; many artistic and/or musical media, e.g. instruments, tapes, songs, etc.

Process: **1.** As a group, read the introductory section to the "Here and Now" exercise from the *Explorations* section of this book.

2. Using a feather or speaking stone, gather participants in a circle and invite each one to tell a story about him or herself, the story of how it feels to be alive in North America at this time in history. All other participants listen without comment, questions or other input. Our purpose is simply to hear what each of us has to say without probing, correction or debate. [The "speaking stone/feather" is an adaptation of a First Nations custom of using a "speaking stick" during meetings of the people. A stick is passed from one speaker to another. As each person holds the stick or stone or feather, he or she "has the floor" and can speak without interruption. The group leader can intervene if the story goes on *too* long. The stone is passed to the next person, and so on until all have spoken.]

3. After each person has had a chance to tell a story, invite everyone to symbolize their experience in some way by drawing or making something and depositing this at a special "altar place" set aside in the room for the purpose.

4. With the expression of "where we're at now," invite participants to think of themselves as empty and open to new experiences, awareness and ideas.

THE USES OF NOTHING

(For groups)

Purpose: To help participants recognize and own their intrinsic powers as human beings, apart from their possession of things or consumption of services.

Materials: Pens, notebooks, markers and flip-chart paper.

Process: 1. Divide participants into groups of five to eight.

2. Select a rapporteur or rapporteuse.

3. Imagine that you are on a tropical island far

from "civilization." You have no tools or other possessions except for your clothing. There is ample fresh water to drink, plenty of vegetable foods for the picking and the climate requires no clothing or special shelter. The island is densely inhabited with plants and animals but none of these present any real danger to human beings.

4. Individually, take a few minutes and list as many activities as you can think of that you could pursue.

5. Next, review these in your group and create a group list. Stimulate and challenge each other to come up with more ideas. The rapporteur should write all suggestions on the flip-chart and tape chart pages to the wall. All suggestions should be charted.

6. When the group list is done, again individually, select your top three preferences based on the personal value of each activity as you perceive it. Ask each person to call out their top three choices and place a check mark beside each nomination. Repeat this for each group member until a cluster of three or four top-rated activities can be identified.

7. As a group, discuss the environmental, economic and human impacts of the top three activities.

8. [Time permitting] Repeat this exercise, assuming that you can bring with you to the island anything that could be purchased for $100 or less.

- *What would you purchase?*
- *How many activities will it add to your list? Be specific.*
- *What effect do these additional activities have on the island environment?*

9. [Time permitting] Repeat the exercise again, this time assuming that you have $10,000 to spend.

- *What would you buy?*
- *How many additional options does it open to you?*
- *How would you rate these options compared to those on your first list?*
- *What are the additional environmental impacts?*

10. Discuss the feelings and results of these exercises:

- *What does our society tell us about the relation between money/consumption/ownership and well-being?*
- *How does this actually square with our experience of life?*
- *What were the relative environmental consequences of lists 1, 2 and 3?*
- *Were the differences in environmental impact worth the difference in reward value, even from a purely human perspective?*

THE COSTS/BENEFITS OF AFFLUENCE

(For groups)

Purpose: To help participants recall past experiences of vitality, satisfaction, joy and reward in life, and relate these to material culture. To what degree has consumerism delivered what it promises? To introduce participants to the concept of the "daily round" and how we spend our time and energy.

Materials: Pens and notebooks.

Process: 1. Have group members read the introduction to "The Best Things In Life..." from the *Explorations* section of this book.

2. Explore the difference between material and non-material culture. As a group, brainstorm as many examples of each as possible and record them on a flip-chart.

NOTE: Compare the length of the two lists. Under which heading can we think of the most examples? Note also how we relate these to ideas of development and underdevelopment, and our assessment of other peoples' cultures.

3. On separate sheets, invite participants to privately recall and record the three "high points" in their lives—moments of maximum well-being, joy and reward. Write a one-paragraph account of each example.

4. Invite participants to select one of these accounts and, through imagination, relive that experience and time. Have group members write extended recollections of these events by suggesting the following stem questions:

- *What were you doing?*
- *Who were you with?*
- *What aspects of this time/experience were most energizing and joyous?*
- *Were there items of material culture essential to make this experience possible? If so, what were they?*
- *What, if anything, prevents you from repeating this experience or others like it?*

5. On a separate page, invite participants to write a paragraph about what they actually do on a typical day. Then discuss this log and the insights that it might bring in response to the following questions:

- *Do these activities bring you reward?*
- *If not, what are they for? What payoffs do they bring?*
- *Are the rewards sufficiently important or necessary to you to continue with this activity?*
- *To what degree does your daily round include activities that are most important to you?*
- *To what extent is your daily round focused on aspects of material culture? What rewards does this bring?*
- *To what extent does your daily round of activity help achieve your goals in life? Is it achieving someone else's goals? Do you endorse these?*
- *Can you imagine any other way to live?*

6. On another page, invite each group member to design a daily round with activities that bring greater reward and meaning to his or her life.

7. When participants have finished writing, allow time for group sharing.

NOTE: This exercise can sometimes evoke strong feelings of "dissonance" for people. The difference between what we value and what we live can be quite wide in modern society and this gap is painful. Normally, this pain/anger/frustration is blocked from awareness through denial, rationalization, or the simple busy-ness of daily routine. The exercise can break through these patterns of avoidance and denial with the result that group members begin to contact their feelings of discomfort. In leading this exercise, it is important that the group leader be skilled and sensitive in dealing with strong feelings in others. As unpleasant as they may be, these emotional pains tell us a great deal about our state of emotional well-being in modern society. Like a wound that has been neglected, the first step to applying effective remedies is recognizing that the wound exists.

I WANT IT NOW!

(For groups)

Purpose: To increase our awareness of our needs as human beings and to distinguish between needs and wants. To help identify the amount of time, effort and energy we expend in pursuit of needs as compared to wants.

Materials: Pens and notebooks, markers, flip-chart paper, tape.

Process: 1. Have group members read the introductory section of the "I Want It Now!" exercise in the *Explorations* section of this book.

2. Form groups of five to eight people. Divide flip-chart paper into four columns.

3. In column 1, as a group, brainstorm and discuss a list of the essential human needs. Include not only the things that are essential to physical survival, but all those things required if a human being is to flourish and reach full potential.

4. In column 2, list the ways in which each need can be fulfilled most directly. Invite group members to record privately in their notebooks how these needs are met in their own lives. Are any going unmet?

5. In column 3, list as many of the environmental

consequences of the way we now try to meet our needs as you can think of.

6. In column 4, for as many examples as possible, invite the group to devise other ways of meeting those needs that have less environmental impact.

7. Set aside the list of needs. Discuss in group the difference between needs and wants. List some examples of wants.

8. If needs are a basic "fact of life" for human beings, where do wants come from? How did we get these ideas?

9. What are the environmental consequences of pursuing wants?

10. Are there other ways of realizing our aspirations that have less environmental impact? If so, how?

11. How much time and by means of what activities do we pursue the fulfilment of wants versus needs?

12. Reflect on those times when you fulfilled a want versus a need. How did you know that a need was satisfied? How do you know when a want is satisfied?

13. If needs are limited by our natural capacities for fulfilment but wants are not, what does this imply for the environment and the ability of others to meet their needs in the future?

14. Pool findings, and discuss. Invite each participant to relate what implications this discussion may have for personal lifestyle.

MY PLANET FOR A CUP OF COFFEE

(For groups)

Purpose: To think about the meaning of progress, diminishing returns, and the displacement of creativity to profit-making goals. To consider the value of things in relation to the needs they serve rather than their market value.

Materials: Pens and notebooks.

Process: **1.** Read Quinn's Coffee Story from the *Explorations* section of this book (*My Planet for a Cup of Coffee*).

2. Invite group members to select some item of material culture that has undergone considerable "development" since it was first introduced, e.g. refrigerators, washing machines, cars, etc.
- *Identify the need this device was created to fulfil.*
- *Trace and record on the flip-chart each stage of its development over the years.*
- *Was there ever a point at which changes in the device failed to produce improvements in its function? If so, when?*

- *What have been the results of the additional changes? Who has benefited from these changes?*
- *Was there ever a point at which development became "overdevelopment"?*
- *What relation exists between this device and the need it is intended to fulfil at the end of its course of development compared to the beginning?*

3. Discuss in group and record your insights.
- *What does this approach to development cost each of us in terms of time, money, the environment, aesthetic quality of life, spiritual peace, international and intercultural understanding and harmony?*
- *What alternatives to this sort of system can we imagine?*
- *What steps can we take immediately to move toward such alternatives?*

LETTER TO DESCENDANTS

(For groups)

Purpose: To help participants feel a sense of the inner continuity of our lives with those of our descendants; to foster a "transgenerational consciousness" that helps connect our present behavior to its future consequences.

Materials: Pens and notebooks.

Process: 1. Read the introduction to the "My Children's Children's Children" exercise in the *Explorations* section of this book. Do guided relaxation and centring.

2. Ask each participant to visualize first themselves, then their own children (nieces, nephews, whomever), then their children's children and finally their great-grandchildren.

3. Once the image of their descendants becomes fully real, ask each participant to write a letter to that child and in the letter to:

a) Tell that descendant how we live in the last years of the 20th century.

b) Write a paragraph or two about what you imagine your great-grandchild's world to be like.

c) Write several paragraphs about what you did during your life to try to prevent ecological disaster. It doesn't matter how successful you think you've been. Just relate what has concerned you, what you wished for, tried to fashion, etc.

4. These letters are entirely private. No one is asked to read from them or hand them in unless they want to.

5. Urge group members to be gentle with themselves. No one person can change the world.

6. Conclude with a paragraph outlining your hopes for your great-grandchild.

7. After writing, allow open discussion time and readings if people wish.

a) How did you feel during this exercise?

b) What insights did you gain?

c) What perspective have you developed on your own lifestyle and its implications for the future?

d) If you experienced some discomfort during the exercise, can you feel this as evidence of connection to a larger, living whole?

NOTE: This exercise can also evoke feelings of dissonance and sometimes of guilt. Therefore, it is important that the group leader handle these feelings with respect and sensitivity. In fact, most of us, most of the time, seldom think much about future generations beyond our own children. This is normal for our culture. When we do take time, however, and consider our connection to future generations and our interest in them, we confront again the narrowness and limitations imposed by the consumerism world view. Most of us *can* feel a strong emotional and spiritual link with the future if we take time and use our imagination to enable the process. It is healthy to feel anger toward a social system that deprives us of this experience of relationship. It is also understandable, though not helpful, to feel some guilt around our past neglect, deliberate or unwitting, regarding this connection. What is most helpful, however, is to experience the reality of our connection with the future and use this awareness to drive new choices of how we spend our time and treasure in the future.

VISIONING A WELL WORLD

(For groups)

Purpose: To discover and connect with the energies of positive imagery. To bring into conscious awareness the inner image of how to live well with the world. To learn to include our sense of a goal worth working toward rather than thinking continually in terms of avoiding disasters. To allow intuition to inform intellect.

Materials: Pens, notebooks, markers, paper, all sorts of craft materials, clays, rocks, etc.

Process: 1. Have participants read the introduction to the "Visioning a Well World" exercise in the *Explorations* section of this book.

2. Invite participants to relax and take a guided fantasy "trip" to a well world of the future. People in this world have learned to live simply, with dignity and with joy:
- *What do neighborhoods look like?*
- *What are people doing to earn a living?*
- *How have cities changed?*
- *What is life like in the countryside?*
- *How does the landscape smell?*
- *What kind of recreation/entertainment do you see?*
- *Etc.*

3. Invite group members to write/sculpt/draw/sing some depiction of their vision.

4. Share visions in the group.

5. On paper now, compare your vision of a well world with our present world as you see it in order to identify two specific actions each group member can take before the end of the week to bring our present world more into line with our visions of simple living.

6. Share these "contracts" and discuss feelings, etc., from the exercise.

Alternate: **5.** After vision-sharing, return to deep relaxation and repeat the steps of visioning. Has your vision of a well world changed on second glance? If so, how?

6. Discuss in group the results of the second round of visioning. Focus in particular on how people in the group feel about each other as a result of sharing visions and revisioning.

7. Do community action contracts as in 5 and 6 above.

Sample workshop agendas

In the next few pages, I offer some suggested group agendas for short workshops on voluntary simplicity. The core plans for workshop activities incorporate the exercises and group experiences described above. Conducting effective workshops requires a relatively specialized set of skills. Experienced group facilitators will feel free to elaborate upon my suggestions and mix and match workshop elements to achieve the desired textures of group experience. Undoubtedly, experienced leaders will also add elements of their own to enrich the whole process.

I believe, however, that study circles and short workshops can be conducted by anyone with some leadership skills, respect for other adults and emotional sensitivity for our common human predicament. Most adults are responsible and autonomous enough to participate constructively in such events. Each group will set its own limits on the depth to which it is prepared to consider the issues and challenges of voluntary simplicity. I would, however, offer just a few suggestions on conducting such workshops.

Place: The places in which we do our work communicate a great deal about the values we associate with that work. There is, for example, something jarringly inconsistent about holding a workshop on voluntary simplicity in a luxury hotel! Participants in such workshops are re-markably sensitive to these inconsistencies. Holding the workshop in a place that reinforces its message will strengthen the entire workshop process. There are many modest retreat houses, nature centres, camps, woodland conference facilities, church and community centres as well as private homes that suit the message of voluntary simplicity splendidly.

Fare: Another feature of workshops that can either reinforce or undermine their central message is what (and how) refreshments and meals are served. Seven-course banquets featuring red meat main dishes contradict the underlying principles of simple living—international and intergenerational equity, ecological sustainability, etc. Elaborate refreshments provided on disposable table service convey the same message. Food *is* important precisely because it is such a powerful focus for human social interaction and is an avenue for our direct, personal and sensuous participation in the goodness of the world. In selecting foods for meals (if your workshop includes a meal) and refreshments, it helps to select simple foods, reusable cutlery and table service, at the same time that we invest some effort in presentation of the food. Simple fare, beautifully presented and appreciatively enjoyed says a great deal about the aesthetics of simplicity and can help reinforce other workshop experiences.

Pace: The pace of workshop activities can be another important element of their effectiveness. Many workshops and seminars now feature jammed work schedules that leave participants exhausted and drained. Group work in service of simplicity should be designed so as to be demanding enough to maintain participants' interest level, but also include times for breaks, socializing and contemplation. This is especially critical for multi-day events. The pace of the workshop process should present an alternative to the manic hyperactivity of many modern "training seminars." The point of exploring voluntary simplicity is not to achieve as *much* as possible in the shortest period of time, but to go *as deep* as possible. This calls for a fundamentally different quality of attentiveness to each other and to the work at hand. Therefore, allow time for people to "soak" in the insights, awareness and new discoveries that come to them through the workshop experience.

Group Work Guidelines: Almost every "workshop" setting evokes associations from our years in public school. Workshops always run the risk of becoming lectures or teaching sessions based on the habits we all absorbed as children. But leading groups of adults in study circles or other group experiences is fundamentally different from managing groups of children in public school settings. Adult learners and group members differ from children in several significant ways:

- Adults bring tremendous experience and expertise to the learning situation partly because of their life experience and partly because they are often already educated in their respective fields of work/interest. Adults, therefore, are not "empty vessels" to be filled up with information (any more than are children!), but are great *resources* to the workshop. The workshop process should aim to draw out the knowledge and gifts of its participants.

- Adults take a pragmatic approach to much of their learning. The relevance that the workshop has to the practical matters of living will therefore be an important ingredient of its success. "Practical matters" are not restricted to the nuts and bolts of budgeting or purchasing decisions. For most adults, depending on their point in the life cycle, issues such as meaning in life, making a contribution to future generations, inner spiritual growth, and participation as productive members of a community are all highly practical issues. The important point is to avoid vague generalities in workshop process. Continually refocus discussion on realistic actions and consequences that relate to personal decisions and commitments as these are lived specifically and concretely in each individual's real-life situation.

- Adults are capable of being highly active in their learning process, although there are certainly passive adult learners. Effective workshop leaders acknowledge that responsibility for fruitful learning rests primarily with the adults in the group. This can be partly achieved by stating up front the expectation that workshop participants are responsible for defining their learning/ experiential goals and seeing that they are fulfilled. Leading adults in workshops then involves not so much directly filling their needs as creating the conditions under which they can fill their own needs (e.g. affirmation, respect, safety, encouragement, rich information resources, adequate time, clear workshop process, flexibility, etc.). Adults tend to resist imposed agendas but will work together to fashion mutually acceptable agendas for group activity. Given these assumptions about workshop participants, I have often found it helpful to distribute some guidelines for group work so that both participants and group leaders can work according to a common set of groundrules. These can be modified or supplemented, depending on the special circumstances of your own group:

—Unless otherwise agreed, all personal information shared in the group is confidential and remains in the group.

—Each group member is responsible for defining his or her goals in participating in the group and working actively and constructively to achieve those goals.

—Every group member deserves respect, sensitivity and consideration. Every person's contribution has value.

—Our goal is mutually respectful dialogue and enrichment. While opinions and beliefs may differ and be in conflict, our purpose is not to debate, to overcome opposition or to convince others of the rightness of our views. We come together to support each other's development.

—Feelings are neither right nor wrong. They are simply facts of our experience that warrant sensitivity and respect. We can be mistaken about matters of fact, but not about feelings.

—We are not necessarily here to reach agreement, consensus or accord. We are all here to support each other in the exploration of territory that may have many different pathways, on journeys with many different schedules. We agree to share experiences we have had on our own journeys.

—We agree to respect the needs and rights of others, maintain the healthfulness and aesthetic values of our workshop surroundings, and claim these rights for ourselves as well.

Sample agenda for a ONE EVENING workshop

7:00 pm   Introductions of participants, group leader(s), and groundrules for group discussion.

7:15 pm   "Circle check" on participants' interest in attending the workshop, their learning goals, and their preconceptions about voluntary simplicity. Chart and display.

7:30 pm   Conduct *Uses of Nothing* <u>or</u> *Costs/Benefits of Affluence* exercise.

9:00 pm   Conduct *Visioning a Well World* exercise.

10:00 pm   Do wrap-up, workshop evaluation, next steps and farewells.

Sample agenda for a ONE DAY workshop

8:30 am   Reception, introductions of participants, group leaders and housekeeping details, if appropriate. Review groundrules for group participation.

8:45 am   "Circle check" on participants' interest in attending the workshop, their learning goals, and their preconceptions about voluntary simplicity. Chart and display.

9:00 am   Session I: *Here and Now* exercise.

10:30 am   *Refreshment break*

10:45 am   Session II: *Costs/Benefits of Affluence* exercise.

12:30 pm   *Lunch* (Provide simple, vegetarian fare that is both delicious and low on the food chain.)

1:30 pm   Session III: *Uses of Nothing* exercise.

3:00 pm   *Refreshment break*

3:15 pm   Session IV: *Visioning a Well World* exercise.

4:45 pm   Do next steps, workshop evaluation, wrap-up and farewells.

5:30 pm   Adjourn.

Sample agenda for a TWO DAY workshop

DAY ONE

8:30 am   Check-in; introductions of group participants and workshop leaders; review of housekeeping details and group work guidelines.

9:00 am   "Circle check" on participants' interest in attending the workshop, their learning goals, and their preconceptions about voluntary simplicity. Chart and display. Review overall workshop plan for next two days.

9:30 am   Session I: *Here and Now* exercise.

10:45 am   *Refreshment break*

11:00 am   Session II: *Costs/Benefits of Affluence* exercise.

12:30   *Lunch*

1:30 pm   Session III: *My Planet for a Cup of Coffee* exercise.

3:00 pm   *Refreshment break*

3:15 pm   Session IV: *I Want It Now!* exercise.

4:45 pm   Review and debriefing of first day.

5:30 pm   *Supper*

Evening: Socializing, contemplation, hiking, etc.

DAY TWO

9:00 am   Dream-sharing (if appropriate); review of day two plans.

9:30 am   Session V: *Uses of Nothing* exercise (extended version).

10:45 am   *Refreshment break*

11:00 am   Session VI: *Uses of Nothing* (continued)

12:00   *Lunch*

1:00 pm   Session VII: *Letter to Descendants* exercise.

2:30 pm   *Refreshment break*

2:45 pm   Session VIII: *Visioning a Well World* exercise.

4:00 pm   Next steps, workshop evaluation, wrap-up, debriefing and farewells.

5:00 pm   Adjourn.

Recommended reading

Babbitt, Dave. *Downscaling: Simplify and Enrich Your Lifestyle.* Chicago, IL: Moody Bible Institute, 1993.

Callenbach, Ernest. *Living Cheaply with Style.* Berkeley, CA: Ronin Publications, 1992.

Conze, Edward. *Buddhist Meditation.* London, U.K.: George Allen and Unwin Ltd., 1968.

Cooper, David A. *Silence, Simplicity and Solitude: A Guide for Spiritual Retreat.* New York, NY: Bell Tower, 1992.

Cox, Connie. *Simply Organized! How To Simplify Your Complicated Life.* Voorheesville, NY: Perie Press, 1988.

Culp, Stephanie. *Streamlining Your Life.* (Out of print.)

Dacyczyn, Amy. *The Tightwad Gazette: Promoting Thrift as a Viable Alternative Lifestyle.* New York, NY: Villard Books, 1993.

Davidson, Jeff. *Breathing Space.* Mastl Press: 1992

de Mello, Anthony (S.J.). *Sadhana: A Way to God.* Poona, India: Gujarat Sahitya Prahash, 1978.

Dominguez, Joe & Vicki Robin, *Your Money or Your Life: Transforming Your Relationship with Money and Achieving Financial Independence.* New York: Penguin, 1993.

Dregni, Meredith Sommers. *Experiencing More with Less: An Intergenerational Curriculum for Camps, Retreats, and Other Educational Settings.* Scottdale, PA: Herald Press, 1983.

Easwaran, Eknath. *The Compassionate Universe: The Power of the Individual to Heal the Environment.* Petaluma, CA: Nilgiri Press, 1989.

Elgin, Duane. *Voluntary Simplicity: Toward a Way of Life That is Outwardly Simple, Inwardly Rich.* New York, NY: William Morrow and Company, Inc., 1993.

Emerson, Ralph Waldo. *Essays and Journals.* Garden City, NY: International Collectors Library, 1968. (See especially the essays on "Self-reliance," "Circles," "Spiritual Laws" and the "Oversoul.")

Enomiya-Lasalle, Hugo M. *The Practice of Zen Meditation.* Bath, U.K.: Aquarian Press, 1990.

Eyre, Richard. *Lifebalance.* New York, NY: Ballantine Books, 1989.

Fromm, Erik. *To Have or To Be?* New York, NY: Bantam Books, 1981.

Hawken, Paul. *The Ecology of Commerce.* Warrenton, VA: Perelandra Press, 1994.

Kabat-Zin, Jon. *Wherever You Go, There You Are: Mindfulness, Meditation....*

Kavanaugh, John Francis. *Following Christ in a Consumer Society: The Simplicity of Cultural Resistance.* Maryknoll, NY: Orbis Books, 1982.

Kirsch, M.M. *How To Get Off the Fast Track....* New York, NY: Harper Collins, 1992.

Lewin, Elizabeth. *Kiss the Rat Race Goodbye.* Walke Press, 1994.

Longacre, Doris Janzen. *Living More With Less.* Scottdale, PA: Herald Press, 1980.

Nollman, Jim. *Spiritual Ecology.* Banpp, 1990.

Rohr, Richard. *Simplicity: The Art of Living.* New York, NY: Crossroad Publishing Co., 1992.

Saltzman, Amy. *Downshifting.* Warrenton, VA: Perelandra Press, 1992.

Schumacher, E.F. *Small Is Beautiful: Economics as if People Mattered.* New York, NY: Harper & Row, 1973.

Shi, David E. *The Simple Life: Plain Living and High Thinking in American Culture.* Uoxft, 1986.

Sinetar, Marsha. *Do What You Love, The Money will Follow.* Mahwah, NJ: Paullist Press, 1995.

St. James, Elaine. *Simplify Your Life.* Hypen Press, 1994.

Study Circles Resource Centre. *The Study Circle Handbook: A Manual for Study Circle Discussion Leaders, Organizers, and Participants.* Pomfret, CT.: Topsfield Foundation, Inc., 1993. (Available from: Study Circles Resource Centre, P.O. Box 203, Pomfret, Connecticut, 06258, U.S.A., (203) 928-2616; fax (203) 928-3713.)

Thoreau, Henry David. *Walden and Other Writings.* New York, NY: Bantam Books, 1989.

Trungpa, Chogyam. *Shambala: The Sacred Path of the Warrior.* New York, NY: Bantam, 1984.

VandenBroeck, Goldian. *Less is More: The Art of Voluntary Poverty.* New York, NY: Harper Colophon Books, 1978.

Wachtel, Paul L. *The Poverty of Affluence.* Philadelphia, PA & Gabriola Island, BC: New Society Publishers, 1989.

Periodicals:

In Context: A Journal of Hope, Sustainability and Change. P.O. Box 11470, Bainbridge Island, WA 98110, U.S.A.

Simple Living Quarterly: The Journal of Voluntary Simplicity. Simple Living Press, 2319, N. 45th Street, Box 149, Seattle, WA 98103, U.S.A.

Essential Living. The Essential Living Society, 409 SE 21st Avenue, Portland, OR 97214, U.S.A.

References

[1] Elgin, Duane. *Voluntary Simplicity: Toward a Way of Life That Is Outwardly Simple, Inwardly Rich.* New York, NY: William Morrow and Company, Inc., 1981, p. 163.

[2] Conze, Edward. *Buddhist Meditation.* London, U.K.: George Allen and Unwin, Ltd., 1968, p. 113.

[3] Lissner, Jorgen. *Personal Lifestyle Response to Social Injustice.*

[4] Lebow, Victor. In *Journal of Retailing.* Quoted in Vance Packard. *The Waste Makers.* NY: David McKay, 1960.

[5] Worley, Michael. Chicago, IL: National Opinion Research Center, University of Chicago, 1990. In Lester R. Brown et al. *State of the World, 1991.* NY: W.W. Norton & Co., 1991, p. 156.

[6] Easterlin, R.A. "Does economic growth improve the human lot? Some empirical evidence." In Michael Argyle, *The Psychology of Happiness.* London: Methuen, 1987.

[7] Progoff, Ira. *At a Journal Workshop.* Los Angeles, CA: Jeremy P. Tarcher, Inc., 1992.

[8] Maslow, Abraham. *Toward a Psychology of Being.* New York, NY: Van Nostrand, 1968.

[9] Simple Living Collective of San Francisco. *Taking Charge.* New York, NY: Bantam Books, 1977.

[10] Hancock, Trevor. "Healthy Cities: The Canadian Project." In *Health Promotion,* Summer 1987.

NEW SOCIETY PUBLISHERS

New Society Publishers is a not-for-profit, worker-controlled publishing house. We are proud to be the only publishing house in North America committed to fundamental social change through nonviolent action.

We are connected to a growing worldwide network of peace, feminist, religious, environmental, and human rights activists, of which we are an active part. We are proud to offer powerful nonviolent alternatives to the harsh and violent industrial and social systems in which we all participate. And we deeply appreciate that so many of you look to us for resources in these challenging and promising times.

New Society Publishers is a project of the New Society Educational Foundation in the U.S., and the Catalyst Education Society in Canada. We are not the subsidiary of any transnational corporation; we are not beholden to any other organization; and we have neither stockholders nor owners in any traditional business sense. We hold this publishing house in trust for you, our readers and supporters, and we appreciate your contributions and feedback.

NSP publishes a number of books that complement this one. For a full catalogue, contact us at one of the addresses below:

In Canada:

In the U.S.A.:

P.O. Box 189,
Gabriola Island, BC
Canada V0R 1X0

4527 Springfield Avenue,
Philadelphia, PA
USA 19143

1065